On Tap
Northern California

On Tap
Northern California

The Essential Guide to Brewpubs and Craft Breweries

STEVE JOHNSON

Foreword by Fritz Maytag

CHRONICLE BOOKS
SAN FRANCISCO

To Fritz Maytag and Jack McAuliffe, California brewing pioneers.

The creation of this book would not have been possible without the assistance, support, and encouragement of friends, family, beer enthusiasts, and individuals in the beer industry. Although too numerous to name all, I would particularly like to thank my wife, Maria, Louis Bregger, Mary Eberhart, and Tom Dalldorf of the *Celebrator Beer News*.

Copyright ©1996 by Steve Johnson. Maps ©1996 by Chronicle Books. All rights reserved. No part of this book may be reproduced in any form without written permission from the publisher.

Printed in the United States of America.

Library of Congress Cataloging-in-Publication Data

Johnson, Steve, 1945-
    On tap northern California : the essential guide to brewpubs and craft breweries / Steve Johnson ; foreword by Fritz Maytag.
    p. cm.
Includes index.
ISBN 0-8118-1066-6
1. Bars (Drinking establishments)—California, Northern—Guidebooks.
2. Microbreweries—California, Northern—Guidebooks. 3. Beer. 4. California, Northern—Guidebooks. I. Title.
TX950.53.J65 1996   95-21384
647.95794—dc20   CIP

Cover design: Brenda Rae Eno
Book design: Pamela Geismar
Illustration: Ross MacDonald
Maps: Françoise Humbert

Distributed in Canada by Raincoast Books
8680 Cambie Street
Vancouver BC V6P 6M9

10 9 8 7 6 5 4 3 2 1

Chronicle Books
275 Fifth Street
San Francisco, CA 94103

Contents

Foreword by Fritz Maytag 7
Introduction 9
All About Beer
    What Are Brewpubs and Craft Breweries? 12
    In the Beginning 13
    What Is Beer? 16
    How Beer Is Made 17
    What Beer Tastes Like .21
    Beer Styles 26

Brewpubs and Craft Breweries

    THE BAY AREA 33

    CENTRAL COAST AND VALLEYS 87

    NORTH COAST AND WINE COUNTRY 105

    SACRAMENTO VALLEY AND THE SIERRA . .135

Beer Festivals 166
Further Reading 167
Glossary 168
Listing of Brewpubs and Craft Breweries 172

Foreword

Fritz Maytag, President, Anchor Brewing Co.

While attending a recent national conference of small-scale and prospective brewers, I was asked whether I had foreseen, in my early brewing days, anything similar to the rapid growth that this segment of the industry has realized in the last ten years.

It would be satisfying to be able to say that I had a clear vision of pub brewing and craft brewing capturing the imagination of American consumers, homebrewers, food and beverage professionals, developers, and even venture capitalists, but though I had great hope, confidence and enthusiasm for the future of this new variety of brewers, I must admit that the immense, widespread acceptance and eager demand for their products still astounds me.

A wonderful wave is sweeping our country: an appreciation of handcrafted beer, made in small batches from the purest ingredients by neighborhood breweries. This burgeoning awareness has had an extraordinary effect on the United States beer industry. There are now more than five hundred craft breweries in the country, all producing specialty beers through traditional methods. These products are most often sold and consumed in close proximity to the brewery, or on-site in the case of a brewpub. A very loyal network of ardent advocates has developed around these brewers, and the message is being transmitted widely by many people—an immense, ad hoc, grassroots force educating more people about the wonder of flavorful, aromatic beers.

As you read this book, more brewpubs and craft breweries are being established in neighborhoods and cities across the nation. Newspapers, magazines, and television and radio stations have become aware of the movement and are increasing public interest and knowledge. Restaurants are installing draft systems, beer lists are being presented as the guests are seated, and multitap bars are appearing all over the country. Beer festivals are increasingly bringing brewers and beer lovers together.

Where will this take us? I am not bold enough to predict, but we do know where it has taken us. Millions of Americans are now demanding and enjoying unique beers made with painstaking care and great devotion by small-scale brewers . . . and that is good.

Another thing that has happened and will continue to happen is that brewers are producing beer and serving it right in their own neighborhoods. I believe this is potentially part of a new attitude toward alcoholic beverages that is sweeping through our country and that will work to the great benefit of everyone. I call this visibility, accountability, and responsibility. By that, I mean that a little brewery, serving its own beers in its own hometown, is visible to its neighbors, accountable to its neighbors, and more likely to be responsible to its neighbors. Certainly, the responsible (and joyous) consumption of alcoholic beverages is what we all are working for in this country, in addition to producing quality beers that uphold the finest traditions of the art of brewing.

INTRODUCTION

This book is written for those who enjoy good beer. If you are among the growing number of beer aficionados, you already understand that a curse has been placed on your head like none ever placed on that of a oenophile. This is because beer is fundamentally different than wine. Wine improves with age; beer does not. In fact, the best place to sample beer is generally at the brewery.

So we beer geeks, as some unkind wit has called us, are faced with the daunting task of visiting the breweries to sample the best beers. But if travel we must, what better place to do it than northern California? This is where the American brewing renaissance began, first in 1965 with Anchor Brewing in San Francisco and then in 1977 with the opening of the now-defunct New Albion Brewery in Sonoma. Since then, more than seventy breweries have opened in northern California. Although surpassed in per capita breweries by Oregon, Colorado, and a few other states, California is where brewers have had the most time to perfect their art.

I tour California breweries from year to year and find the beers improved with every visit. I returned from my first beer tour in 1987 babbling of the wonderful things happening there—tiny breweries in people's garages, brewpubs where you could watch the brewing process take place as you sipped your beer, the dedication of the pioneer brewers and the fantastic beers they were making. As I look back, I realize a lot of the beer I drank was flawed. But I have witnessed the progress made in California and can attest to the high quality and great diversity of area's beers. This is no accident. The creativity, dedication, and hard work of everyone from the brewers to servers has made it happen. California breweries have garnered many awards at the Great American Beer Festival (GABF) held annually in Denver, Colorado. Awards have been noted in the text under entries for individual breweries. For a complete description, see Beer Festivals.

Beer touring is rapidly becoming a popular pastime. But if it were just about tasting beers, it would be a sport practiced by only a handful of fanatics. It is also about developing a camaraderie with fellow beer lovers—getting to know the people behind the beer, sharing the purpose and energy of this burgeoning industry, learning about an ancient craft that has been passed down over the centuries, and, throughout northern California, visiting this beautiful countryside.

Above all else, beer touring is a celebration of diversity. Craft breweries and brewpubs are located in the heart of large cities, on the Pacific coast, high in the Sierra, in small towns, on farms, and even in shopping malls. There is every type of brewery imaginable from the hole in the wall to the fine dining establishment; from brewpubs in shopping malls to brewpubs in isolated villages; from brewpubs with wonderful views to classic wood-paneled saloons; and from sports bars to beer gardens.

So, it is time to begin our beer odyssey. To thoroughly enjoy it, make it as tangible an experience as you can. Chew the grain, smell the hops, sample the brew fresh from the beer tank, kick the tires on the delivery truck, talk to the brewer, chat with other pub patrons, form friendships. Who knows? Maybe you'll even find a personal romance.

All About Beer

What Are Brewpubs and Craft Breweries?

THE BREWPUB

Brewpub is the generic term used to describe an establishment that brews and sells beer for consumption on the premises. Beyond this basic definition there are endless variations on the theme. Some are old and quaint, others modern; some are open and airy, others small and cozy. Some are primarily restaurants, featuring fine dining. Some serve only their own beers, while others may have fantastic selections of draft and bottled beers, substantial selections of wines, or the entire range of alcoholic beverages. However, all brewpubs provide a place where you can relax, socialize, and drink fresh beer, brewed on the premises.

I divide brewpubs into three categories: (1) the true brewpub, (2) the restaurant brewery, and (3) the brewery inn. Many agree that a true brewpub should have a tavernlike atmosphere and be primarily a drinking establishment. A restaurant brewery, as the name implies, places at least equal if not more emphasis on dining. In recent years, the provision of victuals has received increasing emphasis, so much so that the true brewpub has become more difficult to find. In northern California, I would place the following establishments in the category of the true brewpub: Buffalo Bill's, Brewery at Lake Tahoe, Fremont Brewing, Hogshead, Red White & Brew, Rubicon, Triple Rock, Truckee Brewing, and Twenty Tank. The following establishments are clearly brewery restaurants: Black Diamond, Burlingame Station, Faultline, Gordon Biersch, Los Gatos, Pacific Tap, River City, St. Stan's, Santa Rosa Brewing, Stoddard's, Sutter, and Tied House. The rest fall somewhere in the middle. Obviously, these definitions are loose and based on general impressions, not on measurements of the bar and restaurant area, percentage of beer revenue versus food, and so on. I am sure some will disagree with these categories ... and I would enjoy nothing more than to debate this with you over a pint of porter or IPA in any of the above.

The brewery inn is the newest type of brewpub. Simply put, if they brew and serve beer on the premises and provide a bed to sleep in (no, sleeping under a table doesn't count), then it's a brewery inn. Currently, there is only one in northern California—the Calistoga Inn.

THE CRAFT BREWERY

A *craft brewery* is the generic term used to describe a brewery that makes beer using traditional ingredients—malt, hops, yeast, and water—and that doesn't sell beer to drink on the premises.

Another term you will hear bandied about is *microbrewery*, or simply micro. A microbrewery is generally defined as a brewery producing not more than fifteen thousand barrels of beer annually. However, I thought it would seem foolish to exclude breweries making more than fifteen thousand barrels from this guide, especially since some of the finest beers are made by these breweries.

Now that I have clearly defined what is what, let me muddy the waters just a little. Many breweries are both brewpubs and craft breweries, that is, they brew and serve beer on the premises, *and* they distribute to accounts off the premises. Finally, there are *contract breweries*. These are companies that arrange to have their beers made at other breweries. To be included in this guide, a company must own and operate its own brewing equipment, and that equipment must be located in northern California.

IN THE BEGINNING

As we all know, the modern American food and beverage industry prefers to mass produce inexpensive and uniform food and beverage products. Unfortunately, this makes for bland, uninteresting eating and drinking and a lack of choice.

But today, millions of Americans are telling these corporations that they don't want bread that stays "fresh" for a month, chickens grown with hormones, tomatoes that are hard, square, and pink, and beer that has a shelf life of six months. People are willing to pay double or triple the going rate for a product that offers them flavor and quality. It happened with wine, tea, coffee, ice cream, bread, fruits and vegetables, soft drinks . . . and now it has happened with beer.

Because the big breweries refused to produce beer with character, a hardy band of homebrewers, who had become fed up with American beer, were the first to tap this market. Until recently, the large corporations regarded these brewers as dreamers who would never threaten their business. But their shortsightedness has cost them.

A small but growing number of consumers have switched to traditional beer and they are never going back. Just mention the major breweries and they get a bad taste in their mouths. Despite ad campaigns for "ice" beer, "dry" beer, and their ilk, big breweries have permanently lost a segment of the beer-consuming public.

The history of the first modern craft breweries in northern California is interesting, but there is only space here for a sketch. Fritz Maytag was the first visionary to act on his love of good beer. In 1965 he purchased the failing Anchor Brewing Co. in San Francisco. He acted on a whim, which can be a foolish thing indeed. But with hard work, determination, and luck, Maytag turned the brewery around and began to revive long-forgotten beer styles. Though many modern English breweries have kept the traditional names, they have taken the guts out of the beer. Maytag revived some of the original styles which were made in England in *name* only. In this respect, the United States has more traditional and more purist beers than even the English. Anchor has served as a source of inspiration for homebrewers and beer lovers alike.

It wasn't until 1977 that the next step was taken. In that year Jack McAuliffe opened a tiny microbrewery, New Albion, in Sonoma, California. McAuliffe was a homebrewer who had enjoyed many of the traditional ales of Scotland, which he sampled while stationed there in the navy. Though New Albion failed within five years, it served as an inspiration to others, and by the time it closed its doors, microbreweries were popping up all over the West Coast, from southern California to British Columbia. New Albion's brewmaster, Don Barkley, went on to be brewmaster at California's first brewpub.

The next brewery to open in northern California was DeBakker Brewing in Novato in 1979. Brewer/owner Tom DeBakker had been a homebrewer for ten years before he opened his commercial brewery, which lasted until 1981. During those years, DeBakker worked as a fire fighter during the week and brewed beer on the weekends, producing a pale ale and a porter.

In 1980, Jim Schlueter and his wife, Chris Hoover, opened River City Brewing in Sacramento (not to be confused with the current River City Brewing). Schlueter was an ex-Schlitz brewer who felt there was room for craft-brewed lagers. Up to this time, all craft-brewed beers had been top-fermented ales, and he produced a very good, all-malt lager called

River City Gold. Though River City closed within a few years, Schlueter went on to found Hogshead Brewpub in 1986.

In 1981, Sierra Nevada Brewing opened in Chico, California. Two young homebrewers, Ken Grossman and Paul Camusi, founded the company in 1978, but it took them almost three years to raise the money and construct the brewery themselves. They originally brewed Pale Ale, Porter, Stout, and the seasonal Celebration Ale and Bigfoot Barleywine-Style Ale. They have won numerous awards for their beers.

Charles and Diana Rixford began brewing beer in their basement in Berkeley, California, in October of 1981. Their company, Thousand Oaks Brewing, used malt extract and fifty-two-gallon industrial barrels for fermentation. Their four beers—Thousand Oaks Lager, Golden Gate Malt, Golden Bear Malt Liquor, and Cable Car Lager—were distributed in the San Francisco Bay Area. The company is no longer in operation, but some of the beers are still produced by Golden Pacific Brewing Co. in Emeryville.

In 1982 a law was passed allowing brewpubs in California, and the following year California's first two brewpubs and a craft brewery opened. Mendocino Brewing in Hopland was the first, followed within a few weeks by Buffalo Bill's in Hayward. Mendocino's general partner, Michael Laybourn, was able to pick up brewers Don Barkley and Michael Lovett as well as the brewhouse from the failing New Albion Brewery, which had been his inspiration. Laybourn had been a homebrewer for many years. The brewpub opened in the old Hop Vine Saloon and produced ales named after the various birds that inhabit the area. A bottling line was added in 1985.

Owner/brewer Bill Owens of Buffalo Bill's had been a commercial photographer who had developed an interest in brewing. In 1982 he published a book, *How to Build a Small Brewery*. Owens has since opened two more brewpubs in the San Francisco Bay Area and founded two magazines, *American Brewer* and *Beer, the Magazine*. Palo Alto Brewing opened in Mountain View in November. It closed in 1987 after having produced the first batches of Pete Slosberg's beer, Wicked Ale (Pete's beers are now made in Minnesota).

In 1984 Garith Helm and Romy Angle opened Stanislaus Brewery in their backyard on the outskirts of Modesto. They were the first modern brewery in North America to make German altbier. In 1990 the brewery moved to downtown Modesto and reopened as St. Stan's Brewery, a restaurant brewery.

In 1985 Dewayne Saxton opened his Saxton Brewing Co. in Chico. With an award-winning homebrewing background, he fermented in glass carboys. In the same year, Jeff Berrington opened his Redwood Brewery in Petaluma. Both of these breweries were short-lived.

In 1986 Allen Paul, another award-winning homebrewer, opened the San Francisco Brewing Co. in the old Barbary Coast section of San Francisco.

Brewery openings exploded in 1987 with the opening of six brewpubs and two craft breweries—Triple Rock, Tied House, Rubicon, Anderson Valley, Napa Valley, Devil Mountain, Humboldt, Golden Pacific, and Xcelsior. Since then, the rate of openings has continued at a heady pace and shows no signs of slowing down.

WHAT IS BEER?

Beer is a fermented beverage made from cereal grains, water, and yeast. In the modern world it traditionally has been made from malted barley. Other grains used in brewing include corn (from which the South and Central American *chicha* is made), wheat, oats, rye, and rice (from which saké is made). These grains are frequently used in addition to barley to change the character of the beer. In the United States, the use of unmalted corn and rice as adjuncts to malted barley has become almost universal by the larger breweries. Corn and rice lighten the body, diminish the malted barley flavor, and decrease the production costs because both are less expensive.

Fermented beverages can be made from things other than cereal, obviously. Wine is made from fermented fruit. Although some beers have fruit in them, such as the Belgian fruit lambics, these beers are still fermented primarily with malted grain. Hard cider, although popular in many pubs, falls in the wine category because it is made from apples. Mead, made from fermented honey, is neither beer nor wine.

Water, which constitutes up to 92 percent of the finished beer, and yeast, which creates alcohol, are the other two necessary ingredients. The alcoholic strength of beer can range anywhere from less than .5 percent (in the so-called non-alcoholic beers) to a high of around 18 percent by volume. Samuel Adams Triple Bock, brewed by the Boston Beer Co., holds the world record for all beers for alcohol content. Yeast can also give a fruity, or estery, character to the aroma.

A fourth ingredient in almost all modern beer is hops. Hops give bitterness to beer (although over-roasted barley can also do this) and serve to counterbalance the natural sweetness of the malted barley. Hops can also contribute greatly to a beer's aroma, giving it a floral character. Before pasteurization and industrial refrigeration were invented, hops also served as a natural preservative.

Craft brewers tend to be purists. They want their beer to be made with the best ingredients, without adjuncts, additives, pasteurization, or microfiltration. For this reason many of them adhere to the Reinheitsgebot, or German purity law. In 1516 William VI, Elector of Bavaria, declared that only water, malted barley, and hops could be used to make beer. Yeast was not included in the ingredients, as it was taken for granted. The purity law was amended later to allow malted wheat. The Bavarians felt this purity law was so important that they made the continuance of it a condition of their joining the German Republic in 1919. The purity law was struck down in 1987 by the European Court for being protectionist in nature (i.e., not allowing the importation of many foreign beers that contained all kinds of dreadful things). Despite the reversal in the European Court, German brewers have pledged to continue to adhere to the Reinheitsgebot.

How Beer Is Made

There is a lot more to making beer than just throwing some barley and yeast into water and letting it ferment. Beer *can* be made this way, but if you want to brew a particular style of beer consistently, one with an unadulterated flavor and aroma that your customers will learn to like and return for again and again, you will have to be methodical and exact.

Barley must first be malted, dried, and then roasted. This is always done at a malting house, never at the brewery. The way in which barley is roasted affects its flavor. The hops have a very important effect on the beer's nose and palate, and they must be kept fresh if they are to be any good. Water quality can also make a difference to the beer, although some marketing departments for the larger breweries have overemphasized its importance. The type of yeast used (and there are dozens of varieties) can also profoundly influence a beer's flavor.

Finally, beer is very prone to spoilage, caused either by bacteria or wild yeast. All of these things and more can affect the flavor and character of the finished beer. For this reason, brewing has become a very precise science, but one that still allows for the "artist" to express him- or herself in the formulation of recipes.

Once the beer has been brewed, it must be stored and dispensed properly in order to guard against spoilage. Being a very perishable product, if it isn't pasteurized, covered with a pressurized blanket of carbon dioxide, and microfiltered, like the big breweries do, beer begins to decline in quality almost immediately. Like a freshly baked loaf of bread, good beer is delicate and short-lived. The best beer is fresh, unfiltered, unpasteurized, and naturally carbonated. This is what makes brewpubs so attractive. A fresh, well-designed, well-brewed, and well-stored beer is a thing of indescribable yet simple beauty.

THE PROCESS

When you visit a craft brewery or brewpub you will see many tanks, hoses, and other unfamiliar contraptions in the brewing area. The following explanation is designed to provide you with the fundamentals of the brewing process so that you can make some sense of what you are looking at. Many brewpubs label the various tanks, which makes it easier to understand what's going on. But, to make things confusing, different brewpubs use different names for the same piece of equipment. Alternative names are provided in the text that follows.

If you are going to tour a brewery at a time other than when the regular tours are conducted, always call in advance. In fact, it's not a bad idea to let them know you are coming even for a regular tour. Brewing staff are usually happy to accommodate you if they can, but it may be difficult to fit a tour into the brewing schedule.

Malting and Roasting

Malting is a process of steeping the barley so that it will sprout (germinate) and then drying and roasting the sprouted barley. This process converts the starches already present into a more soluble form and activates the enzymes, which are important in the mashing proecess. The barley grains are sorted by size, soaked in water, removed and then spread out and allowed to sprout for about a week.

The malted barley is next dried and roasted in order to arrest the sprouting process. The longer it is roasted in the kiln, the darker and more caramelized the malt will become. This will affect the color and flavor of the beer. The malt is then sieved to remove the barley's roots.

MILLING

Here is where the process typically begins at a craft brewery. Malt is taken from the malt silo, or from bags, and milled (or ground) in a roller mill to produce grist. Milling facilitates the extraction of sugars in the next stage. Some breweries purchase premilled malt, and so begin with the mashing stage.

MASHING

Next, the grist is transferred to the mash tun (or mash-lauter tun) where it is soaked in hot water (about 150°F or 66°C) for one to two hours. The slurry of hot water and malt is called "mash." Mashing converts the starch to sugar and extracts the sugar and other solubles from the grist. At higher temperatures less starch is converted to simple sugars, which makes a sweeter, fuller-bodied beer. At lower temperatures more starch is converted to simple sugars, which produces a drier, lighter-bodied beer.

The mash tun is drained of solubles while remaining sediment is sparged (sprayed) with hot water in order to extract as many solubles as possible. The sweet liquid that drains out through strainer plates in the bottom of the mash tun is called "wort" (rhymes with dirt).

The hot water for the mash is usually, but not always, stored in hot water tanks, called hot "liquor tanks" by brewers. Some brewpubs heat the water for the mash in the brew kettle and then transfer it to the mash tun.

Some brewpubs do not mill or mash their own grains. Instead, they use malt extract, a molasseslike substance, which they put directly into the brew kettle.

BOILING

The wort is transferred to the brew kettle (or copper) where it is boiled with the hops for about one to two hours. Adding hops at the beginning of the boil adds bitterness but very little flavor. Adding hops in the middle or near the end of the boil tends to develop hop flavor and some aroma. And some breweries "dry hop" their beer for extra aroma. In dry hopping, the hops are added during fermentation, or after the boil is finished. The wort is transferred to the whirlpool where unwanted protein, hops, and other solids are separated through centrifugal force. Next the wort is forced to cool rapidly through a heat exchanger (a cooler or wort chiller).

Fermenting

When the wort has cooled, it is transferred to a fermentation tank (also called uni-tank, CIP tank—for "clean in place"—fermenter, or primary), and aerated. The yeast is then pitched (added) to the wort.

Most microbreweries use closed fermentation tanks; however, some use open fermentation vessels, where you can actually see the beer fermenting. At this stage you can see a great deal of foam at the top of the beer. What you can't see is the sediment (called "trub," rhymes with *tube*) forming at the bottom of the tank and the carbon dioxide being released into the air.

Maturing

If the fermenter has a flat bottom, the beer is transferred into a second tank within a few days. If the fermenter has a cone-shaped bottom, allowing the trub to be expelled through a valve in the bottom, the beer can be fermented and conditioned in the same tank. In the conditioning tank (also called bright beer tank, holding tank, finishing tank, or secondary) the beer continues to ferment, but at a much reduced rate. The beer clarifies as small particles settle out and the flavors mature and blend. Conditioning tanks are closed; thus, as the beer ferments and the carbon dioxide can no longer escape, the beer becomes carbonated naturally. Conditioning may take anywhere from a few days to several months. The German lagering method, in which the beer is held for a longer cold-conditioning period, results in a palate very low in yeast effects (i.e., esters), while the ale method, in which the beer is typically matured at warmer temperatures and only for a few days or a week or two, produces a more estery (fruity) beer.

At this point the brewer has the option of filtering the beer before it is served or packaged. Filtration is usually done with diatomaceous earth, which is made up of the microscopic skeletal remains of marine animals and does a very good job of filtering.

Brewpubs usually dispense their beer from serving tanks. Most pump the beer with CO_2 pressure (some with a mixture of CO_2 and nitrogen). If they opt to serve it unfiltered and unpressurized, it is known as "real" beer and can be served with either gravity flow taps or with handpumps.

Kegging and Bottling

An alternative way to package beer is to put it into metal kegs. This way it can be tapped on premise or shipped to another bar or restaurant. Kegging is generally done by adding carbon dioxide under pressure to the keg. Real beer does not use additional carbon dioxide and a wooden peg is placed in the bung, allowing the beer to continue to ferment and condition in the keg. This is sometimes called "cask-conditioned" beer.

In addition, many craft breweries bottle their beers, a more expensive and time-consuming way to package the beer than kegging. Bottled beer from craft breweries is frequently not filtered. Unfiltered beer still has live yeast in it and is said to be "bottle-conditioned." Cask beer and bottle-conditioned beer are much more delicate and perishable than filtered and kegged beer.

Most brewpubs also offer customers their beers in bottles to take home. Usually these bottles have been hand-filled and capped, a very labor-intensive process. Because these beers have been exposed to air during the filling process, I recommend that they be consumed within a few days, if not hours.

Some brewpubs will also fill buckets, jugs, or what-have-you for take out. This beer should be consumed as soon as you get home (but not on the way).

What Beer Tastes Like

If you are confused about how beer should taste, you are not alone. Because our brewing heritage had virtually died out, Americans are having to start from scratch when it comes to beer tasting. To complicate things, some brewers pay little attention to traditional styles when formulating their beers. For this reason, it should be mandatory that every homebrewer who becomes a commercial brewer be given a six-week working vacation to Europe to visit breweries, pubs, and beer halls to find out how the real thing is made and how it tastes. The itinerary should include England, Scotland, Ireland, Belgium, northern France, Germany, and the Czech Republic. Undoubtedly, this suggestion would meet with favor among new brewers.

There are dozens of styles of beer, each one tasting different from the next. It takes time and dedication to become familiar with the style profiles and to learn to recognize them. But it certainly is enjoyable research.

Once you become knowledgeable, you will begin to realize there are three problems that make style identification difficult. First, it is not uncommon for a brewer to apply the wrong name to his or her beer. For this, I will forgive them. I remember trying a thick, malty, sweet ale and telling the brewer how much I liked his Scotch ale. He replied, "That wasn't a Scotch ale, that was a bitter." Could have fooled me!

Second, sometimes a brewer will experiment with recipes, with little thought to style, and then give the beer a name that offers no clue to what style it is. These beers can be the source of interesting though usually inconclusive debates.

Third, there are many beers that are poorly made. When I began drinking imported and craft-made beers, I was thrilled with the different flavors that assaulted my tongue. Later I learned that some of these beers were very poorly made and had flavors that should not have been there. These are known as off-flavors.

For the purpose of analyzing the taste of beer, taste is described in the order that we perceive it. Thus, we have the foretaste (or entry), which is the taste we perceive as the beer enters our mouth; followed by midtaste, the taste we perceive as we swirl or hold the beer in our mouth; and the aftertaste (or finish), the taste left in our mouth after we swallow it.

Finally, remember that everyone's palate is different. Sweet beer to one person may be dry to the second and sour to the third. So don't be a beer snob and tell everyone who disagrees with you that they are wrong. After all, this isn't wine tasting!

To bring out the full aroma and flavor, beer must not be served too cold. Following are suggested serving temperatures for different styles of beers:

Serving Temperatures

ordinary beers	40°F–45°F
quality lagers	45°F–50°F
quality ales	50°F–55°F
quality stouts/porters	55°F–60°F

Major Flavor Components

MALTY: A disproportionately large amount of verbiage has been written about the minor flavors and off-flavors of beer. Little can be found about the major flavor, which is malt. Of course, to be part of the beer intelligentsia, you must never say something like, "Gee, that was a nice, malty beer." That would be like saying *A Portrait of the Artist as a Young Man* is a really good read. Still, identifying the malt is a good start.

Malt tastes like cereal, like cooked grain. It's that delicious aroma you smell at a brewery when the brewer is mashing. If you like that smell, you should love beer. To get a pure, malty flavor or aroma, you want to try a darker beer that is lightly hopped, such as an English brown ale or a Vienna-style lager; many porters, dark lagers, bocks, and Scotch ales can be good examples, too, if not too heavily hopped.

BITTER: Bitterness in beer is usually derived from the hops. It can also come from highly roasted or burnt barley (either malted or unmalted). Bitterness is perceived toward the back of the tongue, so the bitterness comes on stronger near the finish.

HOPPY: In addition to bitterness, hops also impart flavor and aroma to beer. It is possible for a beer to be bitter but not very hoppy, hoppy but not very bitter, and both hoppy and bitter.

Hops impart varying degrees of floral, vegetal, bitter, tangy, spicy, citrusy, piny, and earthy flavors and aromas, and they also counterbalance the sweetness of the malt.

SWEET, DRY: Beers can be either sweet or dry, but most are a combination of both. Beer is sweet because of the maltose from which it is made. The longer beer ferments, the more maltose is consumed by the yeast, and the drier it becomes. Sweetness tends to be perceived in the foretaste, as sweetness is perceived toward the front of the tongue. A normal profile is a sweet entry, followed by increasing dryness.

Other Flavor Components

ALCOHOLIC: This is a warming sensation in the mouth or throat.

CARAMEL: Medium roasted malt and/or boiling a small amount of the wort at a high temperature creates a caramel flavor.

CHOCOLATE: Porters and stouts frequently have a chocolaty character. Even some lagers do, too. This comes from the deeply roasted malt or deeply roasted, unmalted barley.

CLOVY OR BANANA: Cloves or banana is usually smelled or tasted in a weizen bier. This comes from the type of yeast used or warm fermentation. It is frequently considered an off-flavor.

COFFEE: This comes from deeply roasted, unmalted barley, and it's frequently apparent in stouts and sometimes in porters.

ESTERY, FRUITY: A fruity taste comes from the yeast and is frequently noted in fresh, unfiltered ales.

FLORAL: Hops sometimes create a taste and aroma like fresh flowers.

NUTTY: Deeply roasted malts sometimes have a nutty character.

ROASTED BARLEY: This is similar to malted barley but drier and harsher (usually adds a burnt flavor).

SMOKY: Smoked malts impart this taste.

TART: Tart is an acid, slightly mouth-puckering taste, like lemons; it is caused by certain varieties of yeast.

TOFFEE: This is a sweet flavor that is both caramely and nutty.

WOODY: Beer conditioned in wood picks up this taste; in some cases, the brewer may add wood chips to the fermenter.

Off-Flavors and Aromas

Just like bread, beer is a delicate, perishable product, and if not treated properly, it can develop off-flavors very quickly. Beginning with fermentation, all equipment should be squeaky clean, or wild yeast and/or bacteria will develop. Exposure to oxygen promotes the growth of microorganisms and spoilage. Lack of a vigorous fermentation is another cause for bacterial or yeast infection. Fermenting, conditioning, and storing beer at temperatures that are too high also tends to increase the rate of spoilage. Improper pH in the fermenter can promote the growth of bacteria. Light is an enemy of beer also. Off-flavors can develop from beer standing too long on the trub.

Beer will become stale in a matter of weeks or months, so drink it fresh. Cask-conditioned ales, which are unfiltered and have no artificial CO_2 pressure to protect them, should be consumed within a few hours or days from the time they are tapped.

A well-run pub cleans its lines before serving to the first customer. If you ever want to experience the taste of rotten beer, try the first pour of the day from unpurged, unrefrigerated beer lines.

ASTRINGENT: Dry is okay, but astringent makes your mouth pucker.

BUTTERY, BUTTERSCOTCHY: This is unacceptable in a lager, but a certain amount is okay in an ale. The technical term is diacetyl.

CANNED CORN: Caused by improper mashing or boiling or bacteria. The technical term is dimethyl sulfide (DMS).

CARDBOARDY, PAPERY, MUSTY: This is found in beer that is old and oxidized.

GRASSY: Sometimes it can smell or taste like grass or hay. Caused by improperly stored malts; sometimes from hops.

GRAINY, HUSKY: This is a harsh, dry quality caused by mashing for too long or having too high a husk content in the mash.

MEDICINAL: This is like cough syrup. Known in the trade as phenols, these are caused by certain strains of yeast (see under phenolic).

METALLIC: This is a bitter, metal taste caused by improperly cleaned metal surfaces in the brewery.

PHENOLIC: A clovy, bananalike, medicinal, or plastic taste is caused by bacteria or wild yeast (see under medicinal).

SKUNKY: A cabbagy smell, a little like a skunk, is caused by exposure to ultraviolet light.

SOLVENT: Fermentation temperatures that are too high create fusel alcohols, which taste spicy, shellacy, burning.

SOUR, LACTIC, VINEGARY: This comes from bacterial infection, and it's considered a plus at certain levels in a hefe weizen and many Belgian wheat ales.

SULFURY: A sulfur or rotten eggs smell—or if very strong, like a malfunctioning septic system—is caused by hydrogen sulfide. If the beer stands too long on thick layers of trub, it can pick up a sulfury character.

Beer Styles

Beer, like wine, has its styles. In fact, most Americans are surprised to learn that there are more than two dozen major beer styles. Once we add in the classes and subclasses, the number reaches more than fifty. If you are beginning to get the feeling that this is a complex subject, you are right. In fact, several books have been written about beer styles, and entire books have even been devoted to individual styles. The object of this essay is to unlock the mystery of beer styles in as painless a fashion as possible.

There are two basic families of beers: ales and lagers. Ales are more typical of the British Isles, lagers of Germany and Czechoslovakia.

ALES

Ales are made with a yeast that (1) floats to the top of the beer, (2) ferments rather quickly, and (3) works at warmer temperatures than lagers. The brewing process is shorter for an ale than it is for a lager. Because of the shorter and warmer fermentation and conditioning time, ales tend to have a fresher aroma and palate, with a unique fruitiness or yeastiness to them.

LAGERS

Lagers are made with a yeast that (1) sinks to the bottom of the beer, (2) ferments more slowly, and (3) works at colder temperatures than ales. The brewing process is longer for a lager than it is for an ale because lagers go through the lagering process, that is, they condition at cold temperatures for several weeks or months. Lagers tend to be smoother tasting and less aggressive in their character.

The American brewing renaissance has been for the most part a revival of ales. This is because of the hearty flavor of an ale, and because it is more economical to brew an ale, due to its shorter fermentation/conditioning cycle. However, the above descriptions are generalities. Regardless of the yeast used, a brewer can brew a very smooth ale or a very robust lager.

ABBEY ALE: See under Trappist ale.

ALT or **ALTBIER:** This is a dark ale style that originated in Germany before the art of brewing lager developed. It is still popular in Dusseldorf and a few other locales. Altbier comes from the German for "old beer," that is, beer brewed before lager.

AMBER BEER: This term is used frequently in brewpubs and craft breweries to describe beers that are tawny or copper in color. They may be ales or lagers. They tend to be fuller bodied and maltier than their golden-colored counterparts.

BARLEYWINE: A very potent ale, usually full-bodied, dark, and bittersweet. Its strength is typically between 6 and 11 percent alcohol by volume (the "wine" implies that it is as strong as wine). Barleywine and old ale are referred to as strong ales.

BITTER: This is a well-hopped, relatively bitter-tasting ale common to England. The term originated to distinguish the "old" unhopped ales from hopped ales. Bitter is usually served on draft and is amber to copper in color. There are various subcategories of bitter depending on their strengths. These include ordinary, special, and extra special bitter (ESB). The English will be offended if you call it "bitters."

BLONDE ALE: A pale, light-bodied ale, this is also called golden ale.

BOCK or **BOCKBIER:** This style means different things to different people. In Germany it means a strong lager, at least 6.25 percent alcohol by volume. In America the name "bock" has traditionally been applied to dark lagers, at least until Sierra Nevada came out with its Pale Bock in 1990. There is an old wives' tale that bock beer is dark because it is made in the spring when the brewery cleans the dregs out of the brew kettles. There is absolutely no truth to this, and anyone understanding the importance of cleanliness in the brewing process will know that brew kettles are cleaned after every batch. There are two theories as to the origin of the name. One is that it is a corruption of Einbeck, a German city that was once an important brewing center and where the style may have originated. The other theory is that it is a corruption of the German term *ziegenbock*, or "billy goat."

There are many kinds of bocks, including pale bock; Doppelbock (also called double bock or dopplebock), a strong, malty version; Maibock, a pale bock usually served in the spring; eisbock, an extra-strong bock finished by freezing the beer and removing some of the water; and weizenbock, a dark, strong wheat beer. Doppelbocks frequently end with the suffix "-ator" and are easy to identify for this reason. The Paulaner Brewery in Munich started the trend of using the -ator suffix, with its Salvator.

BROWN ALE: There are three subgroups of dark brown ale, based on geographic regions: those produced in southern England are sweet and relatively low in alcohol and hop bitterness; those produced in northeast England are drier but still weak and low in hop bitterness; and those produced in Belgium are stronger and more complex. English brown ales are equivalent to the bottled versions of mild ales.

CALIFORNIA COMMON: This is beer made with lager yeast but brewed at ale temperatures. The style is typified by an amber hue, medium body, and hoppy character. For years it was known as steam beer, but since Anchor Brewing of San Francisco trademarked the name, the term California common was coined to identify the style in brewing competitions. This is the only beer style indigenous to the United States. California common beer originated in nineteenth-century California, where brewers had access to lager yeasts but had no means to keep the beer at the proper temperature. At least two theories persist as to the origin of the name. One is that excessive amounts of pressure built up in the wooden casks, and when they were tapped they made a loud hissing noise, like steam. The other is that steam power was used in the early California breweries, hence the name "steam beer."

CHRISTMAS BEER: This beer is brewed for the yuletide (in Germany, *fest bier*). It is also called holiday beer. It is often dark and relatively high in alcohol, but styles vary widely. Many breweries put herbs and spices in their Christmas beer.

CREAM ALE: This pale, light-bodied ale is lagered at cold temperatures or mixed with lager. It's sometimes called lager ale or "lagale."

DOPPELBOCK: See under Bock.

DORTMUNDER: This pale lager is halfway between a Pilsner and a helles, having more body than a Pilsner, and is less dry as well. It's sometimes called "export."

DRY BEER: Dry beer is made by a special process using enzymal additives in the mash, in which the yeast converts more of the malt sugars into alcohol than normal, making it drier tasting. In Japan, where the first modern dry beers became popular, they tend to be more potent than their counterpart lagers. In the United States, dry beers tend to be of normal strength, but the breweries use lower hopping rates, rendering them almost tasteless. You won't find this kind of beer in a brewpub.

DUNKEL: From the German for "dark," it's any dark lager of average strength. Many bocks are dark, but they are stronger than dunkels. It's also called dunkle, dunkler, Munich or Münchner dunkel, and dunkles.

EXPORT: See under Dortmunder.

FRAMBOISE: See under lambic.

FRUIT BEER: Fruit beer has fruit in it, such as cherries, raspberries, or blueberries. Fruit beer has been brewed over the millenia, but the tradition was kept alive in Belgium. Its popularity has spread to the United States in recent years.

GOLDEN ALE: See under blonde ale.

HELLES: Also called Munich or Münchner helles (from the German for "pale"), Helles is a golden lager that tends to be maltier, less dry, and less hoppy than a Pilsner.

HERB BEER: This is any ale or lager with herbs or spices in it. Many Christmas ales have herbs in them. Common spices used are ginger, nutmeg, and cinnamon.

ICE BEER: Ice beer is frozen just enough to form a few ice crystals, which are then removed. This has little, if any, effect on the taste of the beer.

IMPERIAL STOUT: See under stout.

IRISH STOUT: See under stout.

KÖLSCH: A type of blonde ale brewed in and around Cologne, Germany. This beer tends to be delicate, dry, and fruity. The word "Kölsch" originated from "Cologne."

KRIEK: See under lambic.

LAGER ALE or **LAGALE:** See under cream ale.

LAMBIC: A well-carbonated, spontaneously fermented wheat ale, this beer is very popular in Belgium. There are several varieties, including fruit lambic (kriek—made with cherries, *framboise*—made with raspberries), Faro (a sweet version), and Gueuze (a blend of mature and young lambics).

LIGHT ALE: The meaning of light ale varies. It can refer to (1) the bottled equivalent of an ordinary draft bitter, (2) a low-gravity ale (see page 169 for a definition), or (3) a low-calorie ale.

LIGHT BEER: Light beer refers to either low-calorie, low-gravity beer or pale lager, such as a helles or Dortmunder.

MAIBOCK: See under bock.

MALT LIQUOR: This is an American tax term for a strong beer. Some state laws require that beers above a certain alcoholic strength be labeled as malt liquors. Malt liquors tend to lack character.

MÄRZENBIER: See under Oktoberfest.

MILD ALE: A lightly hopped ale, mild ales are frequently dark in color and low in alcohol.

MILK STOUT: See under stout.

NONALCOHOLIC BEER: Also called alcohol-free or near beer, nonalcoholic beer has less than .5 percent alcohol by weight. However, reformed alcoholics should avoid such beers as they still contain alcohol.

OKTOBERFEST or **MÄRZENBIER:** Originally, this beer was brewed in Germany in March (hence, Märzenbier) and laid down for consumption during the summer and fall. It is ceremoniously consumed in late September and early October. Oktoberfest is amber in color, medium to strong in potency, and malty. It is similar to Vienna, but more robust.

OLD ALE: A medium-strong ale, old ale is usually dark in color, lightly to moderately hopped, and full-bodied. Old Ale and barleywine are referred to as strong ales.

PALE ALE: A copper-colored ale, "pale ale" is a term frequently used to describe a brewer's premium bitter, usually in the bottled form. In recent years it's frequently been used to describe draft bitter. Pale ale is seemingly a misnomer, since there is nothing "pale" about it. The term was originally used to distinguish it from porter, a very dark ale. It is sometimes referred to as Burton ale because it originated in the town of Burton-upon-Trent, England. A slightly stronger and hoppier version is known as India Pale Ale, or IPA. It acquired this name because it was originally brewed for export to India.

PALE BOCK: See under bock.

PILS: See under Pilsner.

PILSNER or **PILSENER**: Frequently referred to as Pils, this is a dry, golden lager originating in Pilsen, the Czech Republic. European-style Pilsners tend to be dry, crisp, and highly hopped, with a floral aroma. Most American premium beers (i.e., from the big brewers) are technically in the Pilsner style, but in character they are mere shadows of their European counterparts. They are paler in color, less hoppy and malty, and have less body. The major American breweries usually substitute corn or rice for a significant portion of the malt, which weakens the malt character.

PORTER: A very dark to black ale, porter originated in eighteenth century London and was first popular among porters (hence, its name). It is traditionally malty and bitter. Many have a dry coffee taste as well. The stronger and more bitter varieties later became known as stouts because (it is said) they were appreciated by the "stoutest" of the London porters.

PREMIUM and **SUPER PREMIUM:** These are price categories used by large American breweries. Premium is usually in the middle price range and super premium is higher priced. These names imply quality, but they have been so misused that craft brewers avoid using them.

RAUCH or **RAUCHBIER:** *Rauch* is German for "smoked" and it refers to beer made with smoked malts. The classic examples come from Franconia, Germany, near Bamberg.

RED ALE: A reddish-colored ale, this beer is sometimes called Irish red.

SCOTCH ALE: This strong, amber to dark, malty, full-bodied ale is originally from Scotland. The stronger versions are sometimes known as "wee heavy." It has also been brewed in Belgium for many years.

SPICED ALE: See under herb beer.

STEAM BEER: See under California common.

STOCK ALE or **STOCK BEER:** This term refers to a strong ale originally brewed to be stored for a long period of time.

STOUT: Stout, a stronger variety of porter, is a very dark to black, full-bodied ale. Two main subcategories exist: dry stout (also known as Irish stout) and sweet stout (sometimes called milk stout because it has lactose—milk sugar—added to it), which is more common to England. In addition there are imperial stout (also known as Russian imperial stout), oatmeal stout, and cream stout. Imperial stout was originally brewed in England and exported to Catherine the Great's court in St. Petersburg. Cream stout is not really considered a style; this term is used in referring to its creamy mouth feel or to its sweetness. Oatmeal stout is made with small amounts of oatmeal to give it body.

STRONG ALE: Potent ales, strong ale is subdivided into old ales and barleywines (the more potent of the two).

TRAPPIST ALE: This ale style was originally brewed by Belgian and Dutch Trappist monks. A true Trappist ale should be relatively strong, use candy sugar in the brewing process, and be bottle-conditioned. They tend to be assertive and complex. Some are full-bodied, with a rich and rounded palate; others are tart and fruity. Stronger versions of the same brand are frequently referred to as "double" or "triple." It's also known as abbey ale.

VIENNA: A reddish-amber lager, usually malty and moderately hopped, this style originated in Vienna in the nineteenth century.

WEE HEAVY: See under Scotch ale.

WHEAT BEER: Any beer using significant portions of malted or unmalted wheat is a wheat beer. There are many styles. Berliner Weisse is an unfiltered, tart, low-alcohol, light-bodied, well-carbonated beer, originally from Berlin. It is frequently served with fruit syrup. Other varieties originating from southern Germany are variously called weizenbier, weisse, or weissbier (*weis* means "white" in German and refers to the beer's very pale color; *weizen* is German for "wheat"). These beers are of a more conventional alcohol strength and body, but they are also tart and fruity. They are frequently served with a twist of lemon. Wheat beers are usually brewed with ale yeasts and malt content varies from 50 to 80 percent. Bottle-conditioned wheat beers are usually called hefeweizen. Other styles include dunkelweizen (dark wheat) and weizenbock, or wheat bock. Wheat beers are generally brewed with ale yeasts. Witbier is a Belgian version of wheat beer with an orangey character and a honeyish aroma.

WHITE BEER: See under wheat beer.

WITBIER: See under wheat beer.

WINTER WARMER: This refers to a beer brewed for consumption in winter that is frequently dark, malty, and fairly high in alcohol, but there are some that are light-colored and emphasize hops instead.

The Bay Area

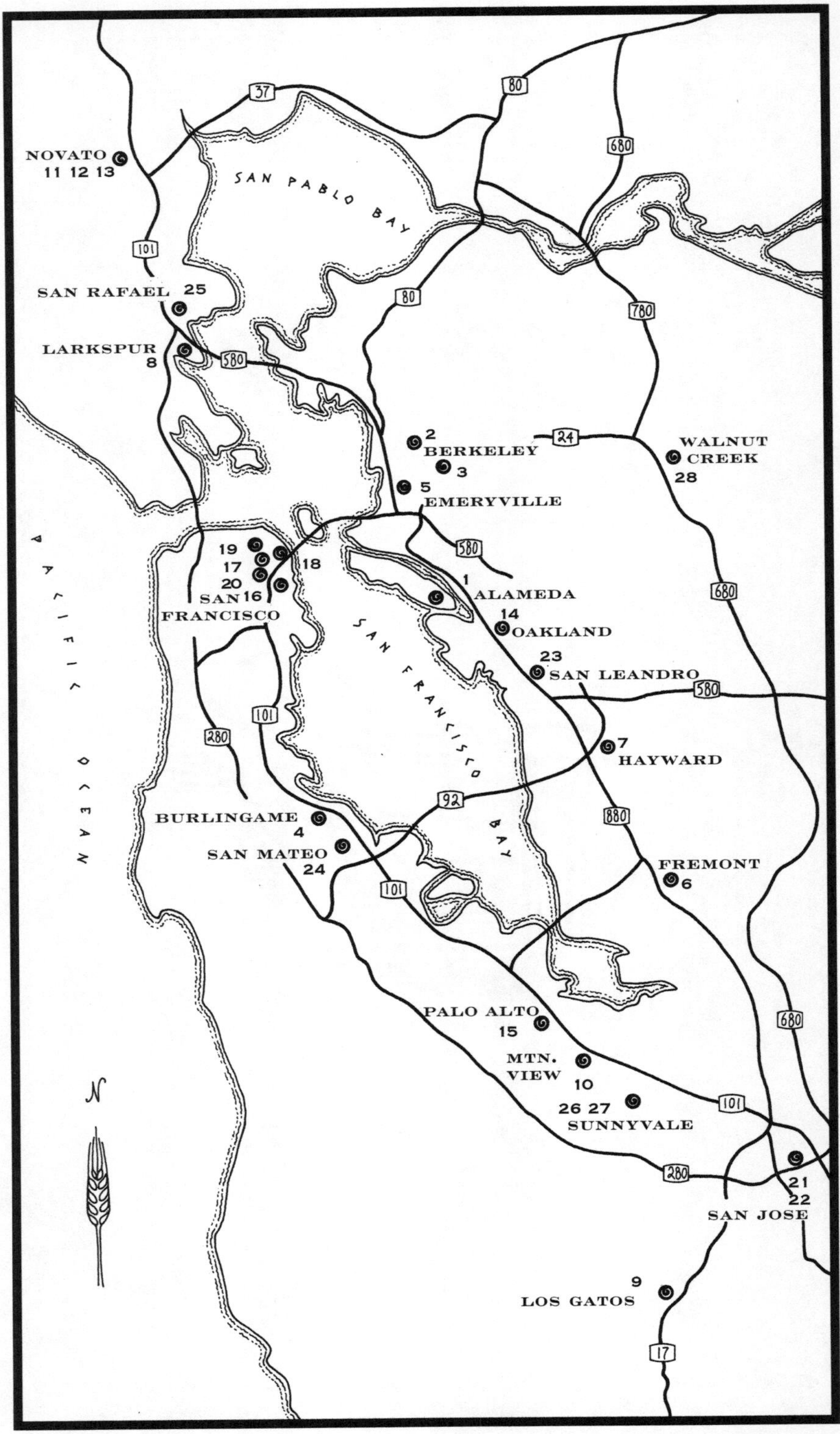

NOVATO
11 12 13
SAN PABLO BAY
SAN RAFAEL 25
LARKSPUR
8
2
BERKELEY
3
5
EMERYVILLE
WALNUT
CREEK
28
PACIFIC OCEAN
19
17
20
18
SAN 16
FRANCISCO
1
ALAMEDA
14
OAKLAND
23
SAN LEANDRO
SAN FRANCISCO BAY
7
HAYWARD
BURLINGAME
4
SAN MATEO
24
FREMONT
6
PALO ALTO
15
MTN.
VIEW
10
26 27
SUNNYVALE
21
22
SAN JOSE
9
LOS GATOS
N
37
80
680
101
780
580
24
280
92
880
17

THE BAY AREA

City	Brewery (Map Key)	Page
Alameda	Tied House Pub & Pool (1)	36
Berkeley	Bison Brewing Co. (2)	38
	Triple Rock Brewery & Alehouse (3)	40
Burlingame	Burlingame Station Brewing Co. (4)	42
Emeryville	Golden Pacific Brewing Co. (5)	43
Fremont	Fremont Brewing Co. (6)	44
Hayward	Buffalo Bill's Brewery (7)	46
Larkspur	Marin Brewing Co. (8)	48
Los Gatos	Los Gatos Brewing Co. (9)	51
Mountain View	Tied House Cafe & Brewery (10)	53
Novato	J & L Brewing Co. (11)	54
	Moylan's Brewery & Restaurant (12)	55
	Pacific Hop Exchange Brewing Co. (13)	56
Oakland	Pacific Coast Brewing Co. (14)	57
Palo Alto	Gordon Biersch Brewing Co. (15)	59
San Francisco	Anchor Brewing Co. (16)	61
	Café Pacifica and Sankt Gallen Brewery (17)	64
	Gordon Biersch Brewery Restaurant (18)	66
	San Francisco Brewing Co. (19)	68
	Twenty Tank Brewing Co. (20)	70
San Jose	Gordon Biersch Brewery Restaurant (21)	72
	Tied House Cafe & Brewery (22)	74
San Leandro	Lind Brewing Co. (23)	76
San Mateo	Barley & Hops Brewery, Blues Club & Smokehouse (24)	78
San Rafael	Pacific Tap & Grill (25)	79
Sunnyvale	Faultline Brewing (26)	81
	Stoddard's Brewhouse & Eatery & Benchmark Brewery (27)	83
Walnut Creek	Black Diamond Brewing Co. (28)	85

Tied House Pub & Pool

8 Pacific Marina, P.O. Box 190, Alameda, 94501

TELEPHONE: (510) 521-4321;
FAX, 521-4890
DIRECTIONS: ON THE ALAMEDA WATERFRONT. FROM OAKLAND, TAKE THE WEBSTER TUBE, TURN LEFT ON ATLANTIC AVENUE, THEN LEFT ON TRIUMPH DRIVE; IT'S AT THE END OF TRIUMPH
HOURS: SUN–THUR: 11:30A.M.–MIDNIGHT; FRI–SAT: TILL 2A.M.
WHEELCHAIR ACCESS: YES
SMOKING: ONLY IN DESIGNATED AREAS
ENTERTAINMENT: LIVE ENTERTAINMENT ON OCCASION, SEVEN POOL TABLES, DARTS
TOURS: CALL FOR APPOINTMENT
CREDIT CARDS: AMEX, DINERS CLUB, DISCOVER, MASTERCARD, VISA

Alameda is one of those quiet bay towns you don't hear much about. San Francisco, Berkeley, Sausalito—yes. But Alameda has lived in anonymity ever since World War II, when it was the point of embarkation for thousands of sailors and millions of tons of navy matériel.

Hidden away in Alameda's waterfront, adjacent to the Oakland Yacht Club, is the Tied House Pub & Pool. The patio is the perfect place to pass the time sipping one of the prolific Tied House beers and enjoying the peaceful view of the yachts in the soft glow of the late afternoon sun. If it is chilly outside, you can still enjoy the view from inside, through the massive glass facade that fronts the yacht basin. In the background, you can hear the quiet click of pool balls coming from the seven pool tables. The view and the seclusion of this spot make it a perfect hideaway in the midst of the hustle and bustle of the East Bay.

The focal point of the Tied House is the main bar with the brewhouse behind it. It sits in the middle of a massive, round room with sky lights and gigantic picture windows. The interior is white with red trim. The floor falls away in curved segments toward the exterior windows, which are just above water level. Pool tables are scattered about. The curved lines, the water, and the color scheme give you the sense of standing in the main ballroom of an ocean liner.

The Tied House is the third in a small brewpub chain operated by the Redwood Coast Brewing Co. The Alameda Tied House opened on December 18, 1991. Although the decor is quite different at each Tied House location, the beers and menu are very similar.

The restaurant offers an extensive menu featuring many items that are either prepared with beer or that complement the beers. They specialize in appetizers, including Oysters Rockefeller, panko calamari, garlic bread with beer cheese, and black bean nachos. Soups, sandwiches, and the famous Tied Burger are offered as well. Entrees include house-smoked baby back ribs, pastas, seafood, house-made sausages, and Idaho trout. Top it off with a gourmet coffee and one of a wide choice of desserts. There is an extensive wine list as well.

THE BREWS

Tied House beers are very gentle beers, providing a needed alternative to the typical, robust ales from northern California. Many people are surprised when they learn that most of the Tied House offerings are ales. Although it is true that the "typical" ale is more robust than the "typical" lager, it is wrong to jump to the conclusion that ales are by definition more robust. It just ain't so, and Tied House is the living proof.

The brew crew here makes quite an array of ales and lagers. The beers tend to be well balanced, slightly fruity, light bodied and shy in their profile. The brewing operation is overseen by Dr. Andreas Heller. A native of Munich, he was trained under the tutelage of the late Cheuck Toms, the original Tied House brewmaster. Heller's able assistant is Jeffers Richardson, graduate of the University of California at Davis masterbrewer's program. Before coming to Alameda, Richardson was head brewer at the Manhattan Beach Brewhouse Grill in Santa Barbara.

The beers are made with a twenty-five-barrel system made by a local manufacturer. All the beers are filtered, except for the wheat beers. Production has increased steadily since opening. By 1994 it had reached three thousand barrels, and Heller expects it to top out eventually at nine thousand barrels. The vast majority of the production is sold to draft accounts throughout Northern California as Redwood Coast Draft.

Tied House beers have taken many awards at the Great American Beer Festival in Denver. The Passion and Dark have each taken gold medals. The Amber, Dry, Pearl Pale, and Dark have all garnered silver medals. Many bronze medals have been won as well.

Normally, eight beers are on tap at all times. Offerings change from time to time, but a fairly complete list would include the following: Tied House Amber Light (1.032), Alpine Pearl Pale (1.055), Berliner Weisse, Ginger, Amber Ale (1.048), Strawberry Amber, Ironwood Dark (1.048), Passion Pale (1.048, made with passion fruit extract), Light Dark, and Tied House Porter.

Bison Brewing Co.

2598 Telegraph Avenue, Berkeley, 94704

TELEPHONE: (510) 841-7734
DIRECTIONS: AT TELEGRAPH AVE. AND PARKER, HALF A MILE FROM THE UNIVERSITY OF CALIFORNIA AT BERKELEY
HOURS: DAILY: 11A.M.–1A.M.
WHEELCHAIR ACCESS: YES
SMOKING: NONSMOKING AREA
ENTERTAINMENT: NIGHTLY JAZZ, BLUEGRASS, CELTIC, AND FOLK MUSIC, POOL, BOARD GAMES
TOURS: BY APPOINTMENT
PARKING: ON-STREET, METERED
CREDIT CARDS: NONE

You're in downtown Berkeley, and you're tired of yuppies and ferns. You want something . . . well, different. Bison Brewing is where it's at.

From outside the glass front, with a view of the tanks, balcony, and wooden framing, Bison Brewery looks pretty tame. Step inside for fun and excitement. From the announcement proclaiming "Poetry and Prose—Open Mic—2nd Tuesday of Every Month" to the loose tobacco near the cash register for those who roll their own to the classic motorcycle hanging from the wall, this place wears a big scarlet letter "A" for alternative. Students, artists, and neighborhood residents make up the clientele, and the establishment seems to be watched over by a set of very hip Muses.

The decor changes as local artists display their work, but the stone-encrusted bar, brew tanks, and David Baker architecture remain the same. Baker designed the windows to look like pictures that need straightening and installed a brass snake sculpture as a railing for the balcony stairs. The brightly painted room is home to a collection of cacti, bags of malt and kegs stacked beside the tanks, and a mural of bent and twisted brew-plumbing behind the tanks. Sit downstairs or go to the balcony, where there are board games and a pool table. There is also an outside balcony for dining with a view of other near-campus shops. The furniture is decidedly eclectic, lending a feeling of relaxed freedom and creative fun.

To cater to the culturally diverse Berkeley campus crowd, the owners use "innovative ingredients and original recipes." The ever-changing menu offers sandwiches such as roasted eggplant, "snakebite" chicken, and teriyaki tofu along with mixed green salads. And, of course, no bar menu would be complete without oven roasted potatoes, homemade peppered dill pickles, and homemade sodas.

The owners are community minded, offering opportunities to taste the wares and donate to local charities at the same time. They provide a place for local musicians to entertain with jazz, bluegrass, folk, Celtic, acoustic rock, and more. Most importantly, they offer their neighbors a comfortable place to enjoy food, beer, music, and each other.

Bison was opened in March 1989 by brewpub entrepreneur "Buffalo" Bill Owens. The brewpub's symbol, an ancient bison transferring the power of Mother Nature to a man, was very apropos. Shortly thereafter, management was transferred to Berkeley graduate Eric Freitag, who along with the brewer at that time set up a cooperative of homebrewers and brew fans and arranged a profit-sharing plan.

THE BREWS

Wouldn't you just know it—this Berkeley brewpub doesn't have any regular beers. That's because head "alchemist" Scott Meyer abides by the overall philosophy of Bison Brewing: create quality through continual change and experimentation. In fact he makes about forty-two different beers a year. He also likes to use unconventional brewing methods, such as sour mashing, partial decoction (a traditional German method of mashing the grain), smoking malts, and fining with oak chips.

Before coming to Bison, Scott made wines at various California wineries and his twelve years of experience shows. Scott does not believe in filtering and occasionally serves up cask-conditoned ales. The bottled beers are bottle-conditioned. He uses a great variety of premilled grains and pelletized hops for his constantly rotating beers. Scott especially enjoys experimenting with unconventional ingredients, such as basil, coriander, chocolate, caramel, honey, and thyme, just to mention a few. Scott's Honey Basil Ale is legendary.

Scott brews with a fourteen-barrel brewhouse and twenty-two- and twenty-eight-barrel fermenters. In 1994, eight hundred sixty barrels of beer were produced. Once a month they get the community involved in the packaging process—volunteers come in to help bottle three hundred cases of beer to be distributed in the Berkeley area.

Three house beers are usually on tap, supplemented by three guest beers and several bottled Bison brews. On my last visit I tried the Coriander Ale, India Pale Ale, and Chocolate Stout. The Coriander Ale had a hazy amber appearance and lots of roasted malt in the mouth with a long, hoppy-herbal finish. It was complex and well balanced. The India Pale Ale was a bright amber to copper and furnished oodles of fresh hops in the mouth. It came on with a herbal, malty palate that evolved to a tangy, hoppy finish. Last on tap was the Chocolate Stout (1.070, made with eight different malts and grains), with a rich chocolate aroma and a turbid, ebony look. The taste was of deeply roasted malt with a note of chocolate (Scott puts fifteen pounds of powdered cocoa beans in the mash). The one bottled beer I tried was the full-bodied Toasted Oat Molasses & Brown Ale (1.066). It was a deep, reddish brown with a tall brown head. It provided a sweet, roasted malt entry, followed by rich malty-molasses and a long, burnt, bitter, roasted malt and coffee finish.

Beer is available for take out in twenty-two ounce bottles and five-gallon and fifteen-gallon kegs.

TRIPLE ROCK BREWERY & ALEHOUSE
1920 Shattuck Avenue, Berkeley, 94704

TELEPHONE: (510) 843-2739; FAX, 843-2856
DIRECTIONS: FROM I-80, TAKE UNIVERSITY AVENUE EAST; TURN LEFT ON SHATTUCK AND IT'S A BLOCK AND A HALF ON YOUR LEFT
HOURS: SUN–WED: 11A.M.–12:30A.M.; THUR–SAT: TILL 1:30A.M.
WHEELCHAIR ACCESS: YES
SMOKING: THERE IS A SMALL SMOKING SECTION
ENTERTAINMENT: JUKEBOX—ESPECIALLY SIXTIES AND SEVENTIES; TV, ANTIQUE SHUFFLEBOARD, DARTS
TOURS: ON A DROP-IN BASIS; GROUPS SHOULD MAKE AN APPOINTMENT
CREDIT CARDS: NONE

To the surprise of no one, Triple Rock was a roaring success from the day it opened in 1986. How could it fail? It provided good beer and good cheer in a tavern atmosphere just a few blocks from the University of California at Berkeley. In fact, I have met more owners of brewpubs who found their original inspiration in Triple Rock than any other brewpub in the country. Since then, owner-brothers Reid and John Martin have gone on to open two other very successful brewpubs—Reid opened Big Time Brewing, just off the University of Washington campus, and John opened Twenty Tank Brewing across the bay in San Francisco. Still, Triple Rock remains both a Berkeley and a national brewpub landmark.

Triple Rock beckons the college crowd with an old-fashioned neon sign on its plain, yellow-brick storefront dating from the 1920s. Inside is a classic saloon with high ceilings and ceiling fans, hardwood floors, windsor chairs, a raised bar with brass foot railing, and antique back bar and walls tastefully decorated with antique beer memorabilia. The brewery can be seen through windows both from the street and in the bar. In the rear is the kitchen and an antique shuffleboard. A tiny beer garden is provided on the roof.

Triple Rock features American pub fare with several kinds of savory, homemade chili, soups, creative sandwiches (including beer-steamed hot dogs), a variety of bar snacks, and daily specials.

THE BREWS

The brewing honors at Triple Rock are performed by brewmaster Jon Paxman, who worked at several breweries before coming here. Jon brews with a seven-barrel JV Northwest system. He uses domestic, two-row pale malt combined with domestic and some British malts, all milled at the brewery. He uses mostly domestic pellet hops, but also Kent Goldings for the cask-conditioned ales, which are dry hopped. The cask conditioning varies from time to time, so check the chalkboard (Thursday night is a good bet for a cask-conditioned ale). The lighter beers are filtered, the darker ones unfiltered. In 1994 about twelve hundred barrels were produced.

Beers are available in ten-ounce ($2.00), pint ($2.50), and pitcher ($8.50) servings. Prices on the specials are usually slightly higher. Sampler sets are available at varying prices, depending on how many are on tap. Usually five to eight beers are on tap, with three regulars and the rest seasonal/rotational. Beer is available for take-out in gallon boxes.

Pinnacle Pale Ale (1.050) is dry and hoppy with roasted malt in the background—it is frequently served on the handpumps. The Red Rock (1.058) is bright amber with a sweet, malt entry and middle and a roasted malt and hoppy-bitter finish. Stonehenge Stout (1.068) is opaque black with a thin brown head, a sweet malty entry, a drying finish, and a deeply roasted malt, espresso palate. Black Rock Porter (1.062) frequently rotates with the stout. Seasonal brews include IPAX IPA (1.060), Tree Frog Strong Ale (1.068), Bug Juice (1.056, traditional English pale ale), Reindeer Ale (1.062, Christmas strong ale), Resolution Ale (1.056, New Years ESB), Century Ale (1.062, strong Scotch ale), Whynot Wheatwine (1.092, wheat wine), Titanium Ale (1.064), Bedrock Barleywine (1.096), and Yak ale (1.054, Scottish export ale).

Burlingame Station Brewing Co.

333 California Drive, Burlingame, 94010

TELEPHONE: (415) 344-6050;
FAX, 344-6097
DIRECTIONS: FROM HWY 101, TAKE THE BROADWAY EXIT; GO WEST AND TURN LEFT ON CALIFORNIA; IT'S ABOUT ONE MILE ON THE RIGHT
HOURS: DAILY: 11A.M.–1A.M.
WHEELCHAIR ACCESS: YES
SMOKING: IN BILLIARDS ROOM (NO CIGARS OR PIPES)
ENTERTAINMENT: TEN WIDESCREEN TVS, BILLIARDS
TOURS: BY APPOINTMENT
CREDIT CARDS: AMEX, DISCOVER, MASTERCARD, VISA

In the spring of 1995, two brewpubs opened in the revitalized downtowns of bedroom communities south of San Francisco. The first to open was the Burlingame Station Brewing Co., which sits directly across the street from the old train station and is now a CalTrain commuter stop. For those flying into California, note that this is the closest brewpub to the San Francisco Airport.

Burlingame Station is housed in what was once the city hall and firehouse, a large, redbrick structure dating to the early twentieth century. The brewhouse is visible both from the street and from the bar area. Inside, the bar-dining room is impressive, with very tall, open-beamed ceilings and an upscale, warehouse look with brick and mahogany walls. As you enter, the polished granite bar sits on your right with mahogany tables in the middle of the room and booths on your left. In addition, there is a large billiards room with six full-size billiard tables and a bar. There is a small beer garden with seating for about thirty.

The kitchen staff prepares many items with beer, including beer-braised sausages, stout creme brulee made with the first runnings from the stout, angel hair pasta with sun-dried tomatoes made with stout, and chocolate porter cheesecake. For lunch and dinner, they offer daily specials, pastas, wood-fired pizzas (the mariner pizza, with smoked salmon, prawns, citrus zest, fresh herbs, and feta cheese is very popular), sandwiches, salads, and appetizers. An extensive wine list is offered as well.

THE BREWS

Teri Fahrendorf, who is the much-awarded brewmaster at the Steelhead Brewery & Cafe in Eugene, Oregon, and is also a partner in Burlingame Station, designed the brewery layout and the principal beer recipes. Curt Anderson, formerly assistant brewer at Bison Brewing in Berkeley, is the brewmaster. After leaving Bison, Curt attended classes at the Siebel Institute in Chicago.

Curt is brewing with a fourteen-barrel brewhouse manufactured by JV Northwest. He uses British and American malts, milled at the brewery. American pellet hops are used. The lighter beers are filtered, with the exception of the Hefeweizen. The dark beers and the cask-conditioned beers are not filtered. The IPA and most of the rotating cask-conditioned beers are dry hopped. Thursday through Saturday nights, two cask-conditioned beers are served on beer engines, and one is usually available throughout the week.

The beers are served in twelve-ounce glasses ($2.50), pints ($3.00), and twenty-three-ounce schooners ($4.25). Cask-conditioned beers are priced slightly higher. Sampler sets of five beers sell for $4.75.

There are four regular beers—Hefeweizen (1.044), Ryegold (1.052, made with 10 percent rye malt), Steelhead Amber (1.052), and Bombay Bomber India Pale Ale (1.059, made with Chinook and Mt. Hood hops). The fifth tap pours the current dark beer from a rotating lineup, which includes McFaddin's Irish Stout (1.054), Station Stout (1.072), and French Pete's Porter, among others. In addition, there are two rotating seasonal beers, including Emerald Irish Ale (1.060), Ryzberry (1.042, fresh raspberry rye ale), Zephyr Alt (1.050), Titanium Wheat (1.072), and many more.

GOLDEN PACIFIC BREWING CO.

5515 Doyle Street, Emeryville, 94608

TELEPHONE: (510) 655-3322; 655-8905

DIRECTIONS: Near the Bay Bridge. From the bridge, take I-80/I-580 north; exit at Powell Street; turn right on Doyle

TOURS: By appointment

Golden Pacific Brewing Co. traces its roots to two breweries: Franklin Brewing and Thousand Oaks Brewing. It was started in 1987 by two University of California at Berkeley students, Ted Strattford and Maureen Lobo. They acquired their equipment from the failed Franklin Brewing Co., which some friends of their had started. Strattford and Lobo distributed their beers in five-gallon beer boxes and twelve-ounce bottles. However, when they left for graduate school in 1990, they left their landlord, David Harndon, with the equipment and he continued with the brewery.

Thousand Oaks Brewing Co. was started in 1981 by Charles Rixford. He and his family made beer in the garage of their home in Berkeley. The beers were made from a base of malt extract and distributed in the Bay Area. In 1990, the Rixfords closed their brewery, and Golden Pacific bought the rights to their beers. Some of the Thousand Oaks brands are still made at Golden Pacific, albeit from all-grain recipes.

The brewery will probably move within the next year, and the owners hope to have a tasting room and offer tours on a regular basis.

THE BREWS

Golden Pacific beers are made by the team of Mark Witty, Alec Moss, and Jim Strickland. Before coming to Golden Pacific, Mark had worked at breweries in England and at the Manhattan Brewing Co. in New York City. Alec and Jim had backgrounds in homebrewing. Jürg Spoerry is in charge of operations.

The brewery has been put together from various sources. It has a fifteen-barrel mash tun/brew kettle and fermenters of various sizes. The beers are made with American, two-row pale malt and American, English, and Belgian specialty malts, all milled at the brewery. American hop pellets are used for seasoning. Some of the beers are dry hopped on occasion. All of the brands are filtered. Output in 1994 was near seven thousand barrels. Eighty percent of the output goes into kegs, which are distributed in the Bay Area; the rest is sold in twelve-ounce bottles.

The brands produced include Golden Gate Ale, Golden Bear Lager, Golden Gate Lager, and Black Bear Lager (available only on draft).

FREMONT BREWING CO.

3350 Stevenson Boulevard, Fremont, 94538

TELEPHONE: (510) 651-5510
DIRECTIONS: FROM I-880, TAKE STEVENSON BLVD. NORTH; IT IS 2 ½ BLOCKS FROM THE FREMONT BART STATION
HOURS: DAILY: 11A.M.–MIDNIGHT
WHEELCHAIR ACCESS: YES
SMOKING: NO SMOKING INDOORS
ENTERTAINMENT: LIVE JAZZ ON MOST WEEKENDS, TV, DARTS, SHUFFLEBOARD
TOURS: ON REQUEST
CREDIT CARDS: AMEX, CARTE BLANCHE, DINERS CLUB, DISCOVER, MASTERCARD, VISA

Fremont Brewing is probably the world's first brewpub located close enough to a golf course to call it the clubhouse. When it opened in 1989, it was called Brewpub on the Green. Another unusual feature—it is a nonsmoking sports bar. You can either stop by after a round of three-par golf or sit in the beer garden and watch other golfers chase that little white ball through the rough and over the greens. Either way, this is a terrific place for a brewery and sports bar.

The inviting brick and wood-framed exterior next to the first tee draws you into the open and airy interior, which is upbeat and modern, with big screen TVs and a U-shaped bar. The light wood ceiling is supported by exposed beams. They boast three satellite dishes with the capability to show every NFL football game. Assorted sports and beer paraphernalia hang from the ceiling, and brick walls set off the booths and collections of trophies.

In the Tap Room, reserved for private dining and parties, a blue marlin watches over festivities. This room is a favorite with local sports celebrities and college booster clubs. The Fremont Wall of Fame displays framed prints of local sports heroes. On Sundays you can enjoy live jazz on the patio.

The menu ranges from pasta and half-pound hamburgers to New York steak. The appetizers are meals in themselves. Try the ploughman's meal—it includes smoked Gouda, French brie, and mild cheddar cheeses, pepperoncini, pickled pearl onions, and the sausage of the day served with a seeded baguette. On the other hand, it would be a shame to miss the killer nachos, the jumbo beer-battered onion rings, or the "Bully-Bully" wings.

For dinner they offer beer-battered cod, Philadelphia cheese steak, a club sandwich, and salads. But then the chicken-garlic fettuccini and the "Brew Plate Special" are worth a try. Whatever the decision, Fremont Brewing Company is worth the trip.

THE BREWS

Brewer Rich Webster began as a homebrewer and has brewed at Fremont Brewing since 1992. He uses a ten-barrel JV Northwest system with two ten-barrel and one twenty-barrel fermenters. American two-row pale and English specialty malts are used. The malt is crushed on the premises. A variety of pellet hops are used, mostly domestic. Many of the seasonal beers are dry hopped. None of the beers are filtered (their philosophy is "filtration is the work of the devil"). About 750 barrels were produced in 1994.

Beers are available in twelve-ounce ($2.25), pint ($2.75), and pitcher ($8.75) servings (the ESB and seasonals are priced slightly higher). Samplers costs $3.25 for five-ounce servings of five or six beers. Beer is available to go in one-gallon cubes.

Mission Wheat (1.046) has a turbid gold look and a malty, fruity palate with notes of fresh hops. Lockout Lager (a California common style) has a honey character. California Amber Ale (1.056) is a hazy amber and is loaded with fresh hops with malt to balance and fruity notes. The ESB (1.072) is a bright reddish copper. It explodes with flavor on the palate, with generous portions of hops and malt and tangy, fruity notes. Mission Peak Porter (1.068) is dark brown with a brown head and smooth, deeply roasted and caramelized malts with notes of chocolate and a delicious, bittersweet finish. Black Cow Stout (1.070) is more aggressive, with a tart, dry palate and a bitter, malty finish. Pumpkin Ale (brewed in the autumn) tastes like fresh pumpkin pie. Other beers include Great Full Red Ale (1.060), Rasperry Wheat (1.046), Independence Ale (1.062), and Spring Fling.

BUFFALO BILL'S BREWERY
1082 B Street, Hayward, 94541

TELEPHONE: (510) 886-9823; FAX, 886-8157
DIRECTIONS: FROM I-880, TAKE A STREET EAST AND TURN RIGHT ON FOOTHILL. THEN TAKE THE NEXT RIGHT ON B STREET. BUFFALO BILL'S IS ON B STREET AT FOOTHILL, ACROSS FROM THE LUCKY SUPERMARKET
HOURS: MON–THUR: 11:30A.M.–11:30P.M.; FRI: TILL 2A.M.; SAT: 10:30A.M.–MIDNIGHT; SUN: 10:30A.M.–9P.M.
WHEELCHAIR ACCESS: YES
SMOKING: NO
ENTERTAINMENT: LIVE MUSIC ON SATURDAY, TV, DARTS
TOURS: DROP-IN BASIS; BY APPOINTMENT FOR LARGE GROUPS
CREDIT CARDS: MASTERCARD, VISA

Hayward, with its relatively small-town atmosphere and tree-lined streets, is home to California State University and Buffalo Bill's Brewpub. This turn-of-the-century Wild West-style saloon is popular with locals and students alike.

The brewpub is named for "Buffalo" Bill Owens, who first opened it in 1983. At the time, it was only the third brewpub to open in the United States. Ever since, Bill, a rootin' tootin' brewery pioneer, has been an outspoken spokesman for brewpubs and has gone on to become publisher of two brewing magazines—*American Brewer* and *Beer, the Magazine*.

Under the watchful eye of the buffalo trophy hanging above the bar, Buffalo Bill's creates an American West sense of fun with hanging globe lamps, wooden bar, and a view of the brewery behind barred windows. The wooden floors, stucco walls and jail cell in the back contribute to the theme. A large neon arrow points to the blackboard listing daily specials, and in season, there might be an occasional pumpkin advertising their Pumpkin Ale.

The menu itself is entertaining. It has the word "beer" written in all of the "major" languages and in several others besides: Rumanian (bere), Swedish (ol), Czech (pivo), Portuguese (cerveja), Japanese (bilru), Swahili (pombe), and Esperanto (biero). They offer a caesar salad with just "a hint of anchovies," nachos, and a plowman's board with aged Cotto salami, sliced cheese, fresh bread, and seasonal fruit. Whatever you get, you will want to try the homemade sourdough breadsticks with a choice of garlic, plain, or garlic and rosemary flavors.

Their personal pizzas are on hand-tossed sourdough crusts. The sandwiches are always served on freshly baked wheat, Odessa rye, or seeded sourdough baguette and include a wide array of deli meats that will satisfy any appetite. Or you might want to try the "Half and Half": half of any sandwich with a half caesar salad—always a favorite.

Whatever you choose, Buffalo Bill's is a great place with good down-home good cookin'. They even have dart boards and live music on Saturday nights.

THE BREWS

Owner/brewmaster Geoff Harries started as a homebrewer who became enamored with the brewing process. He first visited Buffalo Bill's in 1986. After winning several awards for his beers, Geoff decided he wanted to brew professionally. Finding it difficult to secure a brewer's job, in 1991 he began cleaning tanks for free at Buffalo Bill's. After four months of doing this, he became assistant brewer and later became head brewer. Geoff eventually raised enough capital to purchase the business.

Geoff is brewing with Buffalo Bill's original brewing equipment; a small mash tun; a six-and-a-half barrel kettle (scavanged from a dairy farm), two open, horizontal primary fermenters, two Grundies for conditioning, plus serving tanks. Some of the beers are dispensed from kegs.

All domestic malts are used. The pale malt is preground, to which are added specialty malts that are ground with a 1930s coffee grinder. Because the mash tun is much smaller than the kettle, malt extract syrup is added to the boil. The beers are made to a very high gravity—around 1.080—and pure water is added at the end of the boil to bring the gravity down. This method is known as high-gravity brewing and is employed by virtually all of the large breweries in North America. American pellet hops are used for bittering and flavoring, and each beer is then dry hopped with leaf hops—either Cascade or Goldings. Normally four or five beers are on tap—two or three made at Buffalo Bill's (Belle Hop Porter, Buffalo Special Bitter) and two made under contract at San Andreas Brewing (White Buffalo and Pumpkin Ale). None of the beers are filtered. In 1994, the brewery produced about three hundred barrels.

Beers are available in twelve-ounce glasses ($1.75), pints ($2.50), twenty-three-ounce glasses ($3.50), and sixty-ounce pitchers ($8.75). Half-gallon jugs are available for take out.

White Buffalo Ale is hazy gold with a light hop aroma and a predominantly dry, hoppy palate with plenty of malt to back it up. Pumpkin Ale tastes vaguely like a pumpkin pie with vegetal notes. Tazmanian Devil (1.082) is cloudy amber with an off-dry palate of fruit and malt and an alcoholic warmth in the finish. Alimony Ale—claiming to be the bitterest beer in the world—is a hop lover's delight. It is hazy amber with a magnificent, meringuelike head. The fresh, intensely hoppy aroma is followed by an equally hoppy and bitter palate. I would liken the experience to drinking liquid hops. They also brew Special Bitter (1.074), Belle Hop Porter (1.072), and several seasonals. As guest beers they offer Sierra Nevada Pale Ale, Red Nectar, Anchor Steam, Red Hook, and Guinness.

MARIN BREWING CO.

1809 Larkspur Landing Circle, Larkspur, 94939

TELEPHONE: (415) 461-HOPS; FAX, 561-0836
DIRECTIONS: FROM HWY 101, TAKE THE LARKSPUR EXIT AND FOLLOW THE SIGNS FOR THE FERRY (YOU WILL BE ON SIR FRANCIS DRAKE BOULEVARD); IT'S IN THE LARKSPUR LANDING SHOPPING CENTER, ACROSS THE STREET FROM THE FERRY TERMINAL
HOURS: SUN–THUR: 11:30P.M.–MIDNIGHT; FRI–SAT: TILL 1A.M.
WHEELCHAIR ACCESS: YES
SMOKING: NONE
ENTERTAINMENT: LIVE MUSIC ON SATURDAYS AND SUNDAYS, MAY THROUGH SEPTEMBER, TV, DARTS, BOARD GAMES
CREDIT CARDS: AMEX, DISCOVER, MASTERCARD, VISA

Marin Brewing Company is in Larkspur, home of the world-famous San Quentin Penitentiary and the original hot tub. Few people know that it is also a place where wealthy San Franciscans built vacation homes in the late 1800s. Just off San Francisco Bay, Marin Brewing is in the Larkspur Landing Center, across from the ferry terminal, where shops, restaurants, and bay-front buildings entice tourists and locals to come in for a chat, a bite, and a view.

A wood-framed front entrance invites you into a casual, light room with high ceilings, plenty of windows, a mural of Mount Tamalpais painted by Matt Tasley, and collections of beer bottles (with intricate labels designed by Cyd Gibson) and medals won for their excellent brews. Oak floors complement the wooden tables and bar stools. The room is accented with brass, and a fireplace and the wood bar dominate the room; the brewery can be seen behind glass windows. The dining area has a view of the kitchen and the wood-fired pizza oven.

For appetizers, they serve plain ol' bar snacks, such as pretzels, red hot peanuts, pickled eggs, beer-marinated olives, and animal crackers, as well as more sophisticated beer buddies such as ceviche: fresh snapper marinated in lime juice with cilantro, red onion, and serrano chili. For those who like their veggies, Marin offers knishes, caesar, house, and oriental chicken salads, and soup.

For heartier appetites there are sandwiches and hamburgers, and pizza baked in their wood-fired brick oven: spinach pizza also has sauteed mushrooms, calamata olives, ricotta and mozzarella cheeses, tomato, fresh herbs and garlic.

If the trip, whether across land or sea, has made you really hungry, the main courses await. In season, the fresh Manila clams, steamed in amber ale with chili and garlic and served with fresh vegetables and rice are perfect to put you in a coastal California mood. Or you might want to try the trout and spinach: a filet of fresh Idaho trout breaded with cornmeal and deep fried, then served on a bed of fresh spinach sauteed in olive oil and garlic.

THE BREWS

The two general partners in Marin Brewing are Brendan Moylan and Craig Tasley. Craig, with a background in the restaurant business, takes care of the food, while Brendan, who had experience in both beer importing and homebrewing, runs the brewing operation. Brendan was inspired to open his own brewpub when he walked through the doors of Buffalo Bill's Brewpub in Hayward. He describes himself as a "homebrewer gone mad."

The beers are actually made by head brewer Grant Johnston, who went from making bread and cheese into homebrewing. Grant's many homebrewing awards are featured in display cases as you enter the brewery. Alongside them are medals won at the GABF. Marin has won more awards at the festival than any brewpub in the country.

Grant, along with three assistants, brews with a fourteen-barrel system manufactured by Pub Brewing Systems. With up to seven beers on tap at any given time, they have have nine fourteen-barrel fermenters. The grains used are two-row pale and specialty malts, milled at the brewery. A small percentage of wheat is used in most of the beers. Mainstay hops include pellet Chinook, Cascade, and Centennial, but other varieties are also used. The beers are not dry hopped, but generous portions of finishing hops are put into the kettle after the boil. The lighter beers are filtered; the dark beers and hefeweizen are unfiltered. About twenty-six hundred barrels were produced in 1994.

Mount Tam Pale Ale (named after nearby Mount Tamalpais) is the one beer on tap at all times. It is joined by two to six seasonals. Mount Tam sells for $2.00 for a ten-ounce serving, $2.50 for a pint, and $8.00 for a pitcher. Specialty beers cost about 25¢ more. Sampler sets of four four-ounce glasses cost $3.00. There is a retail store with twenty-two-ounce bottles to go. About ten different brands are bottled. The bottles are also available at many retail shops in the Bay Area.

With such a great variety of beers available, mixing beers has become a popular pastime in the brewpub. Some of the favorites have been Black and Blue (Bluebeery Ale and Breakout Stout), Midnight Trail (Breakout Stout and Raspberry Trail Ale), Dark and Fuzzy (Breakout Stout and Peach Ale) and Black and White (Breakout Stout and weiss beer).

Mount Tam Pale Ale (1.055, bronze 1989 GABF) is bright gold, sweet, and malty up front with a fresh, tangy hop finish. Albion Amber Ale (1.058) is bright copper with a roasted malt palate and hoppy finish. Point Reyes Porter (1.065, silver 1991 & 1993 GABF) is dark brown with a rich, roasted chocolate malt palate and a full body. San Quentin Breakout Stout (1.075, gold 1989 GABF) is deep brown to black with a strong, espresso-roasted malt flavor and a bitter, burnt finish. Bluebeery Ale (1.055, gold 1990, 1991, & 1993 GABF) is hazy gold with a light, blueberry fruit aroma and blueberry-malty flavor. Marin Weiss, made with 65 percent wheat malt (1.055, bronze 1989, gold 1991 GABF), is crisp and clean.

Other beers include Marin Hefe Weiss (1.055, gold 1992, bronze 1993 GABF), Hoppy Holidaze Ale (1.070, gold 1990 & 1991 GABF), St. Brendan's Irish Red Ale (1.070), Moylan's Imperial Porter, Miwok Weizn Bock, Old Dipsea Barleywine (1.085, silver 1989 & 1990 GABF), Raspberry Trail Ale (1.055), Marin Doppel Weizen (1.075), Stinson Beach Peach (1.055), and Holy Smoke Harvest Ale (1.068).

LOS GATOS BREWING CO.

130G North Santa Cruz, Los Gatos, 95030

TELEPHONE: (408) 395-9929; FAX, 395-2769
DIRECTIONS: FROM HWY 17, TAKE THE HWY 9 EXIT AND THEN TURN LEFT AT THE FIRST CORNER (UNIVERSITY), THEN TURN RIGHT AT THE THIRD CORNER (GRAYS LANE); IT'S DOWNTOWN ON THE CORNER OF GRAYS LANE AND NORTH SANTA CRUZ
HOURS: SUN–THUR: 11A.M.–11P.M.; FRI–SAT: 11A.M.–2A.M.
WHEELCHAIR ACCESS: YES
SMOKING: NONE
ENTERTAINMENT: TV
TOURS: BY APPOINTMENT
CREDIT CARDS: AMEX, DISCOVER, MASTERCARD, VISA, DINERS CLUB

If you find yourself in Los Gatos, near the Santa Cruz Mountains, take time to look around this tiny, Victorian-era town. Long ago a summer haven for wealthy San Francisco residents and literati (such as John Steinbeck), Los Gatos is now an eclectic mixture of residents, from Silicon Valley computer geniuses to descendants of the original settlers.

Los Gatos Brewing Company beckons from an old building remodeled with stained-glass windows, skylights, a soaring ceiling with exposed trusses, antique pine floors, and rustic, wooden walls with marble accents. It opened in August of 1992, and the owners spared no expense to make this a memorable dining experience. The restaurant is one large room, divided by multilevel dining sections with a view of the exhibition kitchen and the brewery behind a wall of glass. In front of the glass is a mahogany and oak bar, with an arched back bar once belonging to a St. Louis brothel. Dried hop vines add an appropriate adornment. A fireplace is visible from most of the dining area, with a tiled, wood-burning pizza oven to one side. The marble entry was imported from the Old Fillmore Hotel.

The menu rivals the decor for elegance and pleasure. Executive chef Jim Stump offers a menu of delicious variety. The appetizers are as unique as the room itself, offering red pepper and goat cheese timbale with grilled vegetables, New Zealand cockles, and charred tuna carpaccio. Along with caesar and house salads, Los Gatos offers applewood-smoked trout, fresh Asian pears, watercress and grilled radicchio salad, and several choices of pasta. The entrees include scallopine of turkey breast, grilled marinated tuna, baby back ribs (with an apple cider barbecue sauce), and a napoleon of wild mushroom and herb mashed potatoes on a bed of spinach. The lunch menu also offers vegetarian sandwiches, a wood-fired ham sandwich, and a seafood burger with rock shrimp, salmon, sea bass, and tuna.

And the pizza! From that charming, quaint, wood-fired pizza oven comes the most incredible creations this side of New York City. Try the basil pesto pizza, with roasted garlic, fresh tomatoes, and prosciutto, or the spicy chicken with shiitake mushrooms, fresh tomatoes, roasted red peppers, mozzarella and fontina cheese, onions, jalapeños, and cilantro.

THE BREWS

Brewmaster Jeff Alexander and assistant Sherman Thacher are making authentic German lagers on a very large JV Northwest system, which includes a fifteen-barrel brewhouse; two fifteen-barrel and two thirty-barrel fermenters; three forty-barrel lagering tanks; and four fifteen-barrel and two thirty-barrel serving tanks. Jeff apprenticed at a brewery restaurant in the Bay Area after attended brewing classes at the University of California at Davis. In 1993 he opened his own winery—Alexander Cellars—in the Santa Cruz Mountains. Los Gatos brews eight to twelve times a month, and they produced fourteen hundred barrels during 1994.

They use two-row pale and specialty malts from a variety of sources, including domestic, English, and Belgian, and they do their own milling. The predominant hops in the lagers are Northern Brewer from Yakima, Hallertau and Tettnang from Germany, and Saaz from the Czech Republic. The ales use primarily Chinook and Cascade. They offer three regular beers on tap, plus one rotating beer. The regulars include the Lager, Oktoberfest, and Dunkel. Rotating/seasonal beers include Bock, Helles Octaneator (a pale bock), Doppelbock, Hefe Weizen, Pilsener, Pale Ale, Nut Brown Ale, Porter, and Stout. The lighter beers receive an infusion mash; the higher gravity lagers receive a decoction mash (the Pilsener is sometimes infused, sometimes decocted). The Lager and Oktoberfest are filtered; the others are nonfiltered. Beers are available in ten-ounce ($2.00) and fifteen-ounce ($3.00) servings.

The Los Gatos Lager (1.046), made in the Munchner helles style, is very lively indeed, with a bright gold color, a sweet malt entry, and an off-sweet finish with light hops in the background—it took the silver at the 1993 GABF. The Pilsener (1.050) is also very lively with more hop bitterness and a crisper finish. The Oktoberfest (1.054) has a bright copper color and a taste true to the traditional Bavarian Märzen style, with a sweet malt entry, roasted malt in the middle, and a well-balanced malty-bitter finish. For the ale lovers there is an intriguing Nut Brown Ale, which has a hazy auburn color and a soft, yet complex, nutty-malty palate. A Dunkles (1.058) and a Bock (1.074) are also served.

Tied House Cafe & Brewery

954 Villa Street, Mountain View, 94042

TELEPHONE: (415) 965-BREW
DIRECTIONS: FROM HWY 101, TAKE THE SHORELINE BOULEVARD EXIT GOING SOUTH (GOING TOWARD EL CAMINO REAL); AFTER CROSSING OVER THE CENTRAL EXPRESSWAY, TURN LEFT ON VILLA; IT'S ON VILLA BETWEEN CASTRO AND SHORELINE.
HOURS: DAILY: 11A.M.– 1A.M., OR TO CLOSING
WHEELCHAIR ACCESS: YES
SMOKING: ONLY IN DESIGNATED AREAS
ENTERTAINMENT: LIVE MUSIC (USUALLY JAZZ) EVERY FRI AND SAT NIGHT AND SUN AFTERNOON
TOURS: BY APPOINTMENT
CREDIT CARDS: AMEX, DINERS CLUB, DISCOVER, MASTERCARD, VISA

Is there life after computers? To find the answer, a visit to the Tied House in Mountain View is in order. Why Mountain View? Because it lies in the heart of Silicon Valley. Since opening day in January 1988, the Tied House has become a favorite watering hole for people in the computer industry.

To create the Tied House, the owners took a 1920s, warehouselike French laundry and styled it like a California mission on the outside and a German beer hall on the inside. The main room is very large, open, and airy with white walls, a high-beamed wooden ceiling with skylights, and bright red trim on its many windows. It seats up to 225 and also offers a small, trellised patio on one side. On the other side is a display kitchen and brewery. Near the front is a baby grand piano for weekend entertainment.

The Tied House was the brainchild of owner Lou Jemison, who got the idea in 1986 while dining at several brewery restaurants in Baden-Baden, Germany. He found the homemade beer, creative menu, and casual atmosphere to be a winning combination. And it is: Tied House has been brewing to capacity since opening day. In 1991, the parent company, the Redwood Coast Brewing Co., opened two other Tied Houses: one in San Jose and another in Alameda.

The name comes from yet another locale, England. The phrase "tied house" refers to the traditional English system of pub ownership. Tied houses were tied to a particular brewery, either through ownership or through a contractual arrangement, and could only serve the beers from that brewery. Free houses, on the other hand, were pubs that were owned locally and could serve any beer they chose.

For a description of the ample menu, see the Tied House in Alameda on page 36.

THE BREWS

Tied House beers are very gentle beers, providing a needed alternative to the typical, robust ales from northern California. The beers are made with a twenty-barrel system made in Oregon by JV Northwest. All the beers are filtered, except for the wheat beers. Production has increased steadily since opening. By 1994 it had reached three thousand barrels.

Tied House beers have taken many awards at the GABF in Denver. The Passion and Dark have each taken gold medals, while the Amber, Dry, Pearl Pale, and Dark have each garnered silver medals. Many bronze medals have been won as well.

Normally, eight beers are on tap at all times. Offerings change from time to time, but a fairly complete list would include the following: Tied House Light Side (slightly yeasty), Tied House Amber Light (1.032, lightly malty), Alpine Pearl Pale (1.055), Berliner Weisse Ginger, Amber Ale (1.048), Strawberry Amber, Ironwood Dark (1.048, medium dark with a little hop crispness in the finish), Passion Pale (1.048, made with passion fruit extract), Light Dark, Tied House Porter (a delectable brew with notes of bitterweet chocolate), Oktoberfest/Märzen (a fruity version), and Yule Tied.

J & L BREWING CO.
7110 Redwood Boulevard, Novato, 94947

TELEPHONE: (415) 897-3435
DIRECTIONS: FROM U.S. 101, TAKE THE ROWLAND STREET EXIT; LEFT OVER THE FREEWAY TO REDWOOD BOULEVARD
TOURS: BY APPOINTMENT

J & L Brewing—the name really doesn't tell you a lot about the brewery. What does this "J & L" stand for?—Jim Hyde and Lee Strauss, business partners and husband and wife. Jim is a native of San Francisco and Lee is a longtime resident of Marin County.

Jim was a homebrewer for many years before the couple decided to put his brewing skills to the test in 1990, when they put together a three-barrel system scavenged from various sources (primarily from AAA Scrap in Oakland). They set up shop in a warehouse in San Rafael and began producing beers under the San Rafael name. Counter to the national trend, the beers emphasized the malts and downplayed the hops. Over the years Jim has refined his recipes and steadily increased production, from 290 barrels in 1991 to almost one thousand in 1994. In 1992 the brewery moved to Novato, where it coexists with TJ's Bar and

Grill. Although separate businesses, the brewery is visible through windows from the bar and restaurant, and most of the kegs produced at the brewery are served at TJ's. So, after you've toured the brewery, stop by TJ's for some J & L brews.

THE BREWS

Jim and Lee now concentrate on the business side of the the operation, having turned over the brewing to Donald Thornton. Donald began as a homebrewer and is also a freelance tuba player; he frequently plays with the Santa Rosa Symphony. Donald brews six times a week on the original equipment, using premilled, two-row, American pale malts and British specialty malts. The beers are hopped with American leaf hops. The beers are filtered and then kegged or bottled in twenty-two-ounce bottles. Because bottles must be filled the old-fashion way—by hand—the brewery has contracted with Cold Springs Brewing Co. in Minnesota and Golden Pacific Brewing in nearby Emeryville to produce some of the bottled beers.

The brands produced by J & L include San Rafael Golden Ale (1.040, made with 28 percent raw wheat and pale malt), San Rafael Amber Ale (1.045), San Rafael Red Diamond Ale, and San Rafael Stout (1.048), served on draft only.

MOYLAN'S BREWERY & RESTAURANT
15 Rowland Way, Novato, 94945

TELEPHONE: (415) 898-4677
DIRECTIONS: FROM HWY 101, TAKE THE ROWLAND EXIT; THE RESTAURANT IS VISIBLE FROM THE HIGHWAY, ACROSS THE STREET FROM THE MOVIE THEATER
HOURS: SUN–THUR: 11:30A.M.–MIDNIGHT; FRI–SAT: TILL 1A.M.
WHEELCHAIR ACCESS: YES
SMOKING: NONE
ENTERTAINMENT: DARTS, BOARD GAMES
TOURS: BY APPOINTMENT
CREDIT CARDS: AMEX, DISCOVER, MASTERCARD, VISA

Moylan's is Brendan Moylan's second foray into the brewing business. Based on the roaring success of his first brewpub, Marin Brewing, and due to lack of space to expand at that location, he decided to do it again at a new location. Moylan's has the same recipe: good beer, tasty, moderately priced pub grub, and a welcoming and fun atmosphere. The difference is the new brewery has the capacity to produce much more beer, which they are beginning to bottle and keg for distribution throughout California.

Moylan's opened in June 1995. Two large grain silos emblazoned with its logo stand in front of the brewpub, marking the spot for passers-by on the highway. The new building has a stucco exterior and features a pleasant beer garden in the rear, with seating for fifty. Inside you are greeted by a fifty-four-foot bar, the longest in Marin County. This is a place to see and be seen, with a great room housing both the bar and restaurant, with seating for 140. The exhibition kitchen, wood-burning pizza oven, and brewhouse are visible to diners. Wood textures and earth tones combine with the interior design to create a warm and welcoming feeling. To one side is a cozy dart nook with a fireplace and a library. See Marin Brewing Co., page 48, for a description of menu items.

THE BREWS

The beers are made by head brewer Paddy Griffen, an award-winning homebrewer and formerly assistant brewer at Marin Brewing. Paddy brews with a twenty-barrel brewhouse and forty-barrel fermenters. The grains used are two-row pale and specialty malts, milled at the brewery. Mainstay hops include pellet Chinook, Cascade, and Kent Goldings, but other varieties are used also. The beers are not dry hopped, but generous portions of finishing hops are put into the kettle after the boil. The lighter beers are filtered; the dark beers and hefeweizen are unfiltered.

Seven to ten beers are on tap at all times. The standard house beers sell for $2.25 for a ten-ounce serving, $2.75 for a pint, and $8.50 for a pitcher. Specialty beers cost about 25¢ more. Sampler sets of four four-ounce glasses cost $3.00. There is a retail store with kegs and twelve- and twenty-two-ounce bottles to go. The bottles are also available at many retail shops in the Bay Area. One of their first beers was an Irish stout, served under CO_2 and nitrogen pressure. They plan to serve cask-conditioned ales in the future.

PACIFIC HOP EXCHANGE BREWING CO.

158 Hamilton Drive #A1, Novato, 94949

TELEPHONE: (415) 884-2820
TOURS: NO TOURS AT THIS TIME

The Pacific Hop Exchange Brewing Co. went into production on April 24, 1993, using a half-barrel system that was originally designed to do test batches. The beer is then fermented in plastic, food-grade tanks. Their system is so small, brewers Warren Stief and Zachery Shaw are making two batches a day, five days a week. During 1994 they made about 150 barrels.

They are brewing primarily with American and some British malts, milled on site. To this they add American leaf hops, mostly Cascades. The Gaslight Pale Ale is dry hopped. None of the beers are filtered. The beers are distributed throughout the Bay Area in kegs and bottles.

The owners plan to build a much larger brewery in the Bay Area before the end of 1995. In the meantime, they will have some of their beers brewed under contract at the Dubuque Brewing Co. in Dubuque, Iowa.

THE BREWS

The one beer I was able to try was Gaslight Pale Ale, contract brewed at the Dubuque Brewing Co. It is a hazy copper with a fresh hop aroma. It has a sweet, toasty malt entry and middle, and a dry bitter and malty finish with a soft mouth feel. It was very fresh. Other beers include '06 Stout, Graintrader Wheat Ale, and Holly Hops.

PACIFIC COAST BREWING CO.

906 Washington Street, Oakland, 94607

TELEPHONE: (510) 836-BREW
DIRECTIONS: BETWEEN 9TH AND 10TH STREETS, ONE BLOCK WEST OF BROADWAY IN DOWNTOWN OAKLAND
HOURS: MON–THUR: 11:30A.M.– MIDNIGHT; FRI–SAT: TILL 1A.M.; SUN: TILL 11P.M.
WHEELCHAIR ACCESS: YES
SMOKING: NO SMOKING INDOORS
ENTERTAINMENT: JUKEBOX, TV, DARTS
TOURS: ON A DROP-IN BASIS
CREDIT CARDS: DISCOVER, MASTERCARD, VISA

Pacific Coast Brewing Company is in old Oakland, an area of vintage Victorian buildings downtown. Near the convention center, it offers an exciting, upbeat restaurant and brewery frequented by office workers, locals, students, and tourists alike.

The restored 1800s building draws you in with its circa 1912, stained-glass window. When the pub was being restored in 1988, several of the original pieces from the historic Cox Saloon were acquired on permanent loan from the Oakland Historical Museum. It has a unique hand-carved front and back bar and beer cooler and antique beer memorabilia. The wood wainscot enhances the exposed brick walls, wooden floors, and glass doors that lead to the redwood-enclosed beer garden, decorated with lush, green vines. The brewing process is visible downstairs. Worth watching for are festivals—spring beer tasting, anniversary party, Halloween costume party, Christmas beer tasting, tailgating, a pub crawl, and the New Year's party.

The menu includes traditional fare such as hamburgers, chili, pizza, and a wide selection of sandwiches. There is also a ploughman's platter of sausage, cheese, and apple with a baguette. The delicious salads include a spinach and smoked chicken and a caesar. For something really special, Pacific Coast presents the Cornish Pastie, a pastry stuffed with beef, potatoes, and vegetables and served with real mashed potatoes, gravy, and vegetables.

Pacific Coast Brewing Company is the place to go for a little history served up with flavorful food, a pleasant atmosphere, and excellent beverages, all at reasonable prices. In fact, if Oakland is not on your agenda, you should plan a side trip. It is well worth the visit.

THE BREWS

Brewmaster Don Gortemiller first got into brewing in 1975 after he was given a homebrew kit by his college fraternity brother and future partner in the brewpub, Steve Wolff. He says it "kind of got out of control after that." The brewing is done with a seven-barrel system obtained from the defunct Palo Alto Brewing Co. The beers start with a base of malt extract, and depending on the type of beer being brewed, specialty grains are added. Don uses the high-gravity method—the wort is made very thick and then pure water is added at the end of the boil. A combination of American pellet hops (such as Chinook, Nugget, Centennial, Willamette, Perle, and Columbus) is then added. Primary fermentation takes place in closed, flat-bottom tanks. From there, the beer is racked into secondary fermenters and, finally, into seven-barrel Grundies serving tanks. Leaf hops are frequently added in the secondary fermenters (dry hopping), as well as oak chips. The beers are fined with isinglass and served unfiltered. In 1994, they produced 450 barrels.

Normally, four house beers are on tap, plus fifteen guest beers (all craft-made). Beers are served in ten-ounce glasses ($2.00) and pints ($3.00). Samplers are available. Five-gallon kegs are available for take out with a five-day advance notice.

Grey Whale (1.050) is a classic English pale ale. It's clear gold with a big, dry malt palate balanced with fresh, hoppy bitterness (bronze 1991 GABF). Blue Whale Ale (1.070) is a deep, burnt orange Scotch ale. It starts out very fruity and malty, nutty and sweet in the middle; it finishes very long, bitter and hoppy-resiny with an alcoholic warmth—very complex, full bodied and delicious (silver 1989 GABF). Pilgrim's Pride Maple Brown Ale is fruity with lots of caramelized malt. It is made with real Vermont maple syrup. Humpback Alt (brewed in the fall) is smooth and well balanced with a hoppy finish (bronze 1990 GABF). Killer Whale Stout (1.054) is dark and roasty with chocolate overtones (silver 1990 GABF). Other beers include Amethyst Ale, Mariner's Mild (1.040) and Imperial Stout (silver 1992 and 1993 GABF), Belgian Triple (bronze 1994 GABF), Columbus IPA (the first beer in the country using all Columbus hops), Emerald Ale (Irish red ale), Yellow Jacket Ale (light honey beer), Blue Code Barleywine, and Holiday Strong Ale (in bottles only).

GORDON BIERSCH BREWING CO.

640 Emerson Street, Palo Alto, 94301

TELEPHONE: (415) 323-7723;
FAX, 323-6129
DIRECTIONS: FROM HWY 101, TAKE THE UNIVERSITY AVENUE EXIT. IT IS LOCATED DOWNTOWN, A BLOCK AND A HALF SOUTH OF UNIVERSITY AVENUE.
HOURS: SUN–THUR: 11A.M.–11P.M.; FRI, SAT: 1P.M.– MIDNIGHT
WHEELCHAIR ACCESS: YES
SMOKING: ONLY IN BAR AREA
ENTERTAINMENT: TV
TOURS: BY APPOINTMENT
CREDIT CARDS: AMEX, DINERS CLUB, MASTERCARD, VISA

Pop quiz. What do the Kingston Trio, Stanford University, and the Gordon Biersch Brewing Co. have in common? They all started in Palo Alto. So, after touring the campus and listening to an old Kingston Trio album, stop by Gordon Biersch on tree-shaded Emerson Street downtown to check out the brews.

In 1988 Dan Gordon and Dean Biersch opened Gordon Biersch, their first restaurant brewery, in the old Bijou movie theater. After experiencing instant success in Palo Alto, breweries have spread to San Jose, San Francisco, Pasadena, and Honolulu.

The term "brewpub" is taboo to owners Dan and Dean. They envisioned their place first and foremost as a restaurant, second as a brewery, and never as a brewpub. To their credit, they have done a magnificent job with the design, decor, beer, and food.

Gordon Biersch has a high-tech, chic look, featuring an exhibition kitchen with a spectacular view of the glassed-in brewery. Local artists display their work on the walls, and all art is for sale. On one wall are handsome, locked mahogany cabinets in which members of the mug club keep their mugs.

Visitors enjoy the open, airy atmosphere created by the high ceilings—complete with ceiling fans—track lighting, and more subtle, indirect lighting with a grain motif. The bar area walls are light with wood trim and glassed archways. While the soaring ceiling gives the impression of vast spaces, small tables, with upholstered stools and crystal vases (filled with sprigs of barley), encourage intimate conversation.

Dean Biersch brings twelve years of restaurant and hospitality experience to the Bay Area. He and his master chefs have designed an international, eclectic menu with selections from the Southwest to the Mediterranean and from Asia to Germany. Presentation is the name of the game here and just the sight of the dishes will make your mouth water. Not to be missed are the Prince Edward Island mussels, steeped in broth laced with Märzen beer; or for a more continental experience, try the jaegerschnitzel with braised red cabbage and roasted red potatoes. Appetizers include the usual light fare with a twist. Try garlic fries, Thai chicken skewers, or grilled prawns. The full menu offers a range of pasta dishes, fresh seafood, meats, salads, and homemade desserts. And where else could you find Chocolate Decadence: a whipped cream mousse topping a sliver of chocolate, floating on raspberry puree.

Close to the Stanford University campus, Gordon Biersch attracts a crowd as eclectic as its menu. So, pull up to the granite bar and enjoy the total experience.

THE BREWS

Masterbrewer Dan Gordon, with the assistance of masterbrewer Tom Davis, supervises the brewing operations at all five of the Gordon Biersch breweries. Dan was the first American in over thirty years to graduate from the rigorous, five-year brewing engineering program at the Technical University of Munich in Weihenstephan. Michael Ferguson is in charge of the operations at Palo Alto. With a background in electrical and mechanical engineering, he was brought in to keep the old German brewing equipment running. He was trained as a brewer on the job by Dan and Tom.

Michael does consecutive brews in a twenty-barrel brewhouse. The mash is done in the traditional German decoction manner. The wort then goes into forty-barrel fermenters. A combination of American, German, Canadian, and English malts are used, depending on the brew. Authentic German Hallertau Hersbrucker hops are used. In 1994 production reached fourteen hundred barrels.

Three beers are on tap at all times—Export, Märzen, and one rotating beer. The rotationals include an unfiltered Dunkles, an unfiltered Doppelbock around Christmas, and a Maibock in the spring. The Export, Märzen, and Dunkles are served in ten-ounce ($2.00) and half-liter glasses ($3.50). Specialty beers are slightly more expensive. Kegs are available for take out in 2.5-, 5-, and 15.5-gallon kegs—please call ahead if you'd like one.

Even though I am an ale fan, I must admit that the Gordon Biersch lagers are delectable. The Export has a pleasant, sweet malty entry and a crisp, hop finish—a good quaffing lager. The Märzen is a dark amber, very smooth with a subdued, roasted malt finish that's balanced with mild hop bitterness. The Dunkles is a tasty brew, with a complex, roasted malt character and a hoppy bitterness in the background. I think I like the Dunkles the best, but it's a difficult choice.

If you would like to receive an intensive tour of the brewery, drink some authentic German beer, and even have lunch with the brewer, then you'll want to attend the monthly Brewers Lunch. It costs $25, and please make your reservation far in advance.

ANCHOR BREWING CO.

1705 Mariposa Street, San Francisco, 94107

TELEPHONE: (415) 863-8350
DIRECTIONS: FROM MARKET STREET, TAKE 7TH STREET SOUTH TO KING STREET, TURN RIGHT; KING ENDS ON DEHARO, WHICH YOU FOLLOW TO THE CORNER OF MARIPOSA, IN THE POTRERO HILL DISTRICT
TOURS: BY APPOINTMENT ONLY—CALL FOR DETAILS. TOURS ARE HIGHLY TECHNICAL, AIMED AT THOSE WHO ARE KNOWLEDGEABLE ABOUT BREWING

This is it—the brewery that started the craft brewing movement, the spark that ignited the explosion, the Plymouth Rock of brewing. But if you want to drop to your knees and give thanks to the pioneers who brought back our brewing heritage, don't end your pilgramage here. Mosey on over to 541 Eighth Street, where the brewery was located when the revolution got under way.

A bit of history. Fritz Maytag, of the appliance family, first discovered Anchor Steam Beer™ as an undergraduate at Stanford University in the late fifties. He and his buddies usually drank it at a bar in Menlo Park called the Oasis. He liked the beer's hoppy-bitter character and became a fan of Anchor Brewery. But Anchor Steam was unavailable in the bottle and not many restaurants carried it on draft. Besides tasting different from the national brands, it was produced by one of the few remaining local breweries in the nation.

Very little is actually known about steam beer's predecessors. It is fairly clear that around the turn of the century "steam" was used as a kind of nickname to describe a number of beers on the West Coast that were apparently produced under widely varying conditions and with a broad range of ingredients. By definition, these beers would have differed greatly from brewery to brewery, as well as from batch to batch. For many decades only Anchor has used the quaint name "steam" for beer, and it is a registered trademark of Anchor Brewing Company.

There are many theories as to where "steam" beer got its name. The most common is that the casks made a steamlike hissing noise when tapped, due to the high pressure that built up inside. Another theory is that some of these early breweries employed steam to heat the brew kettles and steam engines to power the brewery. Still another is that the beer was put outside to cool at night, and it would steam in the cold air. Then there is the story of the brewer named Pete Steam . . . and on and on.

The breweries making steam beer gradually closed, as did almost all regional and local breweries across the nation. By 1965, Anchor was the only brewery left making steam beer, which brings us back to Fritz Maytag.

Maytag stayed on at Stanford in graduate school studying Japanese. One night, shortly after completing his studies, he was dining at the Olde Spaghetti Factory in the North Beach neighborhood. The restaurant owner told him he had better enjoy his glass of Anchor Steam because the brewery was closing by the end of the week. Maytag was disturbed by the demise of such a dearly beloved institution and decided to visit the brewery in order to pay his respects. On his visit, he met the president and sole employee, Lawrence Steese. Steese, like Maytag, had been a fan of Anchor Steam Beer and had purchased the brewery in 1958 in order to save it from extinction. Despite Steese's efforts, the product was inconsistent and sales continued to decline. After a lengthy conversation, Maytag bought a controlling share in the brewery for $5,000.

When Maytag bought the brewery it was producing less than seven hundred barrels a year. He describes it as one of the most primitive breweries in the world and the butt of many a joke in the industry. The brewery had no refrigeration, no control of carbon dioxide, and used baker's yeast instead of cultured brewer's yeast. There was no bottling line, and the racking system was a rat's nest of pipes and tubes. Sales continued to dwindle until 1969, when Maytag bought the brewery outright, rolled up his sleeves, and went to work to put it back on its feet.

For a time, Maytag was the only full-time employee, and he did everything, from making the beer to delivering it. On more than one occasion, as he was trying to market his beer to potential customers, he was told the brewery had closed years ago. Although Maytag knew almost nothing about making beer, he set out to make traditional beers using modern equipment. He worked in the brewery by day and studied the science of brewing by night.

The brewery slowly recovered. Much of the old equipment was cast off in favor of new equipment. In 1971 bottling began and production rose to twelve hundred barrels. In 1974 a new product, Anchor Porter, was introduced. Up to that point, Anchor was the only American brewery producing an all-malt beer. In 1975, Anchor brewed Liberty Ale to commemorate Paul Revere's ride. With Liberty Ale Anchor became the first modern American brewery to dry hop beer. In doing so, it created the first modern American pale ale. But 1975 was important for another reason: Anchor turned a profit for the first time in a decade.

That Christmas, a slightly modified version of the Liberty Ale became the first Our Special Ale, Anchor's Christmas beer. Anchor continues to release a different version of Our Special Ale around Thanksgiving. Two years later Anchor released Old Foghorn, the only commercially available barleywine made in America at that time.

In 1979 the brewery moved to its present location on Mariposa Street, in an old Chase & Sanborn coffee plant. That same year, production reached twenty thousand barrels. The new brewery has flat, open fermenters and a 110-barrel brewhouse made by Ziemann, moved from a small brewery in Karlsruhe, Germany.

Anchor continues to increase production and to introduce new beers. In 1984 Anchor Wheat was introduced; in 1989, Ninkasi; and in 1992, Anchor Spruce Beer. In 1994 production passed the hundred-thousand-barrel mark.

THE BREWS

Anchor Steam Beer is an all-malt beer that is hopped with Northern Brewer leaf hops. It is fermented in two-foot-high flat fermenters and then warm fermented for an additional three weeks. Before it is packaged, it is krausened and then flash pasteurized. The color is a medium copper, and it has a faint, fresh, fruity aroma. The palate is of caramel malt with a satisfying, hoppy-bitter finish.

Anchor Wheat has a light body and palate. It is clean, crisp, and refreshing. The Wheat is only available on draft.

Liberty Ale has a hazy, deep, gold to amber color with a creamy head. The pungent aroma of fresh hops foretells wonderful things to come. It explodes in your mouth with fresh Cascade hops and has an extremely long, flavorful finish. I make no secret that this is one of my favorite beers. It took a silver medal at the in the IPA category at the 1993 GABF.

Anchor Porter is opaque brown-black with a tall, dark brown, creamy head. It has a rich, fruity, chocolate-roasted malt palate, a bittersweet finish, and a full body. An earlier version had coffee notes in it, but the new version has more of a chocolate tone.

Old Foghorn is one of those beers to die for. It is a deep copper with a fine, creamy, tan head. The fresh, hoppy-malty aroma is inviting. The palate is complex, with both hops and roasted malts competing for your attention, and it has a sturdy body. The finish is ambrosial with all of the previously noted complexity, plus an alcoholic warming sensation in the mouth. It took a gold medal in the barley wine category at the 1991 GABF.

Our Special Ale varies slightly each year. It is usually very complex with several kinds of malts and hops, plus herbs and spices to make it even more interesting. It won a bronze medal in the herb/spice category at the 1993, a silver in 1992, and a bronze in 1991.

CAFÉ PACIFICA AND SANKT GALLEN BREWERY

333 Bush Street, San Francisco, 94104

TELEPHONE: (415) 296-8203; **FAX:**, 296-9348
DIRECTIONS: IN THE FINANCIAL DISTRICT, CORNER OF MONTGOMERY STREET
HOURS: MON–FRI: 11A.M.–10P.M.; SAT, SUN: 11A.M.–9:30P.M.
WHEELCHAIR ACCESS: YES
SMOKING: ONLY IN BAR AREA
TOURS: BY APPOINTMENT
CREDIT CARDS: AMEX, DINERS CLUB, MASTERCARD, VISA, DISCOVER, CARTE BLANCHE

Okay. You've experienced every kind of dining adventure the Bay Area has to offer, right? Not if you haven't visited the Café Pacifica and Sankt Gallen Brewery! This gem of a brewpub is buried at the ground level of the "333 Bush Street" building in San Francisco's financial district. It packs a big surprise into just a few square feet.

This dim sum restaurant and pub combines Asian cuisine with California ales. The atmosphere is quietly elegant, with recessed lighting, framed, matted prints, Japanese antiques, and classical and jazz music. The modern architecture is a restful contrast with the cacophony of the streets. With its sharply sloped ceilings drawing the eye to recessed nooks where sculptures are nestled, Café Pacifica gives the illusion of being more spacious than it is. The bar area overlooks the glassed-in brewery, while the dining area offers a view of Bush Street from the windows.

The dining area, with only eight tables and forty-eight seats, is one of the smallest brewpubs in the world. It is located behind Japanese screens and offers a menu one step up from the traditional dim sum specialties: they use fresh ingredients, faster cooking preparation, and lighter oils to create the most delicious assortment of dim sum on the West Coast. Dim sum means "touch of the heart" and that is just what they are. Try such delicacies as tulip chicken drummettes, jade dumpling, shumai, Cantonese sweet rice, and Chinese szechuan bun. The small portions of food are ordered three to five dishes at a time. And don't forget the desserts! Almond tofu, sesame cookies, snow balls, and chestnut cream sweet buns finish off any meal with a touch of elegance. Lunch combinations are available until 3:00 P.M. or you may order from the dinner menu.

THE BREWS

Brewer/owner Kozo Iwamoto, a native of Japan, was so inspired by the art of brewing that when he opened his brewpub in March of 1993 he named after the ancient monastery of Sankt Gallen (Saint Gall) in Switzerland. Here are found the oldest written records of brewing in Europe, dating back to the eighth century. In the centuries that followed, the monks of Sankt Gallen brewed beer for their daily enjoyment and offered it to the monastery's guests.

Kozo makes about three batches of ale a month using a seven-barrel brewing system manufactured by DME Brewing Services. He uses all domestic malts and pellet hops. All of the ales are filtered. In 1994 about 250 barrels were produced. The three ales are available in twelve-ounce glasses ($2.95) and sixteen-ounce ($3.75) glasses. A set of samplers costs $3.00.

The Pale Ale is a bright gold with a fresh but subdued hop aroma. The palate has a pleasant, fresh, dry hoppy character. The Amber Ale has a roasted malt character with a fairly long, well-balanced, bitter finish. The Dark Ale has a rich nut brown color with a subtle, yet complex, deeply roasted malt personality.

Gordon Biersch Brewery Restaurant

2 Harrison Street, San Francisco, 94120

TELEPHONE: (415) 243-8246; FAX, 243-9214
DIRECTIONS: ON THE EMBARCADERO, NEAR THE BAY BRIDGE
HOURS: SUN–WED: 11A.M.–11P.M.; THUR–SAT: TILL 1A.M.
WHEELCHAIR ACCESS: YES
SMOKING: SMOKING DOWNSTAIRS, NONSMOKING UPSTAIRS
TOURS: BY APPOINTMENT
CREDIT CARDS: AMEX, DINERS CLUB, DISCOVER, MASTERCARD, VISA

Where is a great place to sit at night and look at the lights of the San Francisco Bay Bridge, or to watch fireboats and sailboats during the day? Gordon Biersch Brewery Restaurant! In fact, the upstairs dining room offers one of the best views of the bay that the city has to offer. Head down toward the water near the bridge and look for the corrugated steel grain silo at 2 Harrison Street. This is the only outside advertisement you will find with the brewery's name.

The building is the old Hills Brothers Coffee Company, and it still features the neon coffee sign on the roof. The interior isn't your typical warm-wall, dark-wood establishment. It is modern, bright and breezy, full of energy and fun. From the restaurant balcony upstairs you can look down to the bar and brewery below, but you will probably be too enchanted looking through the windows at the bay and bridge to do so. On the other hand, you may be distracted with the clientele—the best and the brightest converge on the establishment all day and long into the evening. True aficionados will want to watch the brewing from the U-shaped bar area downstairs, highlighted with wrought-iron, mahogany-topped tables, where you can order from the café menu. Wherever you are, there is never a boring minute or a dull view.

For a description of the menu, please see Gordon Biersch in Palo Alto (page 59). But it bears repeating that Dean Biersch has brought a wealth of restaurant experience to his design of the wonderful, international-cuisine inspired menu, which offers such delicacies as warm goat cheese salad and beer-steamed clams and mussels. There are appetizers to satisfy any wild cravings, from Thai chicken skewers and Buffalo wings to garlic fries. The only bad thing about the menu is trying to make a decision.

First opened in March 1992, the Gordon Biersch Brewery Restaurant is part of the revitalization of San Francisco's SOMA district. Its atmosphere fits comfortably between white tablecloths and fast food—offering the elegance of gourmet dining without a dress code. There is an energy about the place that seems to draw you in from the street.

THE BREWS

Next time you see a tanker truck driving across the Bay Bridge, better pay it a little respect—it might contain wort from Gordon Biersch Brewing. Some of the batches from the brewhouse are sent to the Gordon Biersch facility in Emeryville, where they are fermented, aged, and packaged for sale to other bars and restaurants. This arrangement was worked out because there was an increased demand for their product but no room for expansion at the San Francisco facility.

So why is there such a demand for Gordon Biersch beers? Because they are authentic German lagers. Brewmaster Dan Gordon supervises the brewing operations at all five of the Gordon Biersch breweries. When the San Francisco Gordon Biersch opened, Dan brought in John Berardino. John had apprenticed at Vernon Valley Brewery in Vernon, New Jersey, and later had worked at the Brauhaus Castel in Mainz-Kastel, Germany. He says he has received many positive comments about his beers from German tourists who stop by the brewery.

John does consecutive brews in a twenty-five barrel brewhouse. The mash is done in the traditional German decoction manner. The wort then goes into fifty-barrel fermenters. A combination of American, German, Canadian, and English malts are used, depending on the brew. Authentic German Hallertau Herbrucker hops are used. They brew about eight times a week and age the beer four to six weeks before serving. In 1994 production reached thirty-six hundred barrels.

Three beers are on tap at all times—Export, Märzen, and one rotating beer. The rotationals include an unfiltered Dunkles, an unfiltered Doppelbock around Christmas, and a Maibock in the spring. The beers are served in ten-ounce ($2.50) and half-liter ($3.50) glasses. Kegs are available for take out in 2.5-, 5-, and 15.5-gallon kegs—please call ahead to reserve one.

The Export is a bright gold with a slightly sulfury aroma. The palate has a pleasant maltiness with light hops in the background. The Märzen has a nice, bright copper color and a medium-roasted malt palate. The Dunkles has a reddish brown color and an attractive creamy head. The palate is of roasted malts—smooth, yet complex.

For an intensive tour of the brewery and lunch with the brewer, plan to attend the monthly Brewers Lunch. It is held the third Saturday of each month and costs $25. Please make your reservation far in advance.

SAN FRANCISCO BREWING CO.

155 Columbus Ave., San Francisco, 94133

TELEPHONE: (415) 434-3344
DIRECTIONS: AT THE CORNER OF COLUMBUS & PACIFIC
HOURS: MON–THUR: 11:30A.M.–12:30A.M.; FRI: 11:30A.M.–2A.M.; SAT: NOON–1:30A.M.; SUN: NOON–MIDNIGHT
WHEELCHAIR ACCESS: YES
SMOKING: THERE IS A SMALL SMOKING SECTION
ENTERTAINMENT: LIVE JAZZ FOUR NIGHTS A WEEK; TV, DARTS, BOARD GAMES
CREDIT CARDS: AMEX

As you enter San Francisco Brewing through the handsome oak doors, the clock turns back to 1907, just after the great earthquake and the year this classic bar first opened as the Andromeda Saloon. It was a showplace in its day in a section of town that was known as the Barbary Coast, made famous by sailors and miners who caroused and debauched to their heart's content. In the early days, Jack Dempsey was the bouncer at the saloon—he later went on to be world heavyweight boxing champion. Mobster Baby Face Nelson was captured here by the FBI in 1939. The Andromeda eventually closed, reopened in 1977 as the Albatross Saloon, and closed again.

The old saloon was rediscovered in 1985 by Allen Paul, an award-winning homebrewer and resident of the nearby North Beach neighborhood. Alan had been looking for a place to build San Francisco's first brewpub. In it, he discovered the perfect building to combine a modern brewpub with the history and culture of San Francisco.

The brewpub is located on the edge of several San Francisco neighborhoods and affords easy access from all. To the south is Chinatown and the financial district. To the north is North Beach, an old Italian community now known for its nightlife. During the fifties this neighborhood was the center of the Beat Generation with the likes of Ginsberg and Kerouac frequenting the local coffeehouses and City Lights Bookstore, just down the street from the brewpub.

As you enter San Francisco Brewing, large, stained-glass windows frame the big oak door—almost as if you were entering a church. To your right is the main showpiece, an antique mahogany bar trimmed in brass with an ornate backbar of mirrors framed by rosewood columns. At the base of the bar is the typical brass foot rail and an untypical tile trough spittoon. Overhead, running the length of the room, is the famous "oompah" fan—paddles made of wood and palm fronds that radiate from a slowly turning iron axle, providing more ambiance than fresh air. On the opposite wall hangs an enormous antique clock—perhaps the largest I have ever seen in a bar—above a large display case of California beer memorabilia. The room is completed with old photographs of San Francisco and a vintage piano.

Directly ahead and up the stairs is the Jack Dempsey room, a cozy den with a dart board and a view of the bar below. At the end of the bar and around to the right is the small Brew House Room. It has an old black-and-white tile floor, small tables with bentwood chairs for diners, and a kitchen. The room offers diners not only a view of the intersection of Columbus and Pacific through plateglass windows, but a glimpse of the brewhouse to one side. The rectangular, stainless steel mash tun sits on a platform high above the diners. Below is the handsome, solid copper brew kettle. The fermentation and conditioning takes place in the basement.

The pub specializes in freshly made pub fare with many appetizers, salads, sandwiches, several burger entrees, fish and chips, and roast chicken.

THE BREWS

The beers are made by brewmaster Allen Paul and head brewer Mark Stein on a seven-barrel system that was manufactured locally. They use primarily American malts and leaf hops, with some English and European specialty malts and hops added. The Pony Express Ale and the Shanghai IPA are dry hopped. All of the beers are served unfiltered. In order to let the beers settle properly, after the initial week of fermentation, they are aged for an average of three weeks. In 1994, one thousand fifty barrels of beer were produced.

Usually four to six beers are on tap in servings sizes of ten ounces ($2.75), pints ($3.25), and pitchers ($11.50). One-gallon brewcubes are available for take out.

Albatross Lager is hazy gold with a robust and complex, malty-hoppy palate, some sour and buttery notes, and a dry finish. Emperor Norton Lager is a dark amber and also has a complex, malty palate with some buttery and sour notes. (Incidentally, this beer bears the name of a local merchant who lost his marbles after going bankrupt and in 1888 dubbed himself Norton I, Emperor of the United States and Protector of Mexico; he wandered this section of San Francisco wearing a military uniform and sword.) Barbary Coast Brown is dark, reddish brown with a pleasant, roasted malt palate. Pony Express Ale is copper colored with a roasted barley palate and a hoppy-tangy finish. Gripman's Porter is dark brown with a bittersweet, malty palate accompanied by rich coffee notes and a full body. Russian Imperial Stout has a pleasant, sweet, deeply-roasted malt palate and a bittersweet chocolate finish that warms the throat. Other beers include Brew House Stout, a very fresh and hoppy Shanghai IPA, Grace Darling Bock, and Andromeda Wheat Beer.

TWENTY TANK BREWING CO.

316 11th Street, San Francisco, 94103

TELEPHONE: (415) 255-9455
DIRECTIONS: SOUTH OF MARKET, BETWEEN FOLSOM AND HARRISON
HOURS: DAILY 11:30A.M.–1:30A.M.
WHEELCHAIR ACCESS: YES
SMOKING: SMOKING SECTION
ENTERTAINMENT: LIVE JAZZ THREE NIGHTS A WEEK, TV, JUKEBOX, DARTS, SHUFFLEBOARD
CREDIT CARDS: CARTE BLANCHE, DINERS CLUB, MASTERCARD, VISA

You're in the big city, it's late at night, and you're looking for an alternative to glitzy night clubs and cocktails. How about some super suds and lively conversation in comfortable and unpretentious surroundings? Then head into Twenty Tank Brewing in trendy SOMA.

Beneath the five-foot, neon beer mug, and beyond the bronze-framed glass entrance is an experience not to be missed. The unique Frank Lloyd Wright-era design of the entrance draws you into the spacious early-twentieth-century interior, sporting pressed tin walls, exposed ductwork, steel beams, and brass-trimmed glass lamps suspended from the two-story ceiling. These wonderful lamps once graced the men's department of the old Roos Department Store on Market Street. The dark wood floors and bar and the iron balcony railing bring a warmth to the warehouse-style bar, which is enhanced by steel kegs and, of course, the now more than twenty fermenting and serving tanks at the rear. The stainless-steel brewing equipment is visible behind glass walls. Adorning the walls are early 1900s-style beer posters, designed by local artist Barbara Flores, with winsome beauties advertising Twenty Tank's contemporary brews, including Old Scout, Hi-Top, and Red Top. A neon lettered clock, advertising the brewpubs' own Kinnikinick brand, keeps time while rock music provides the background for lively conversation.

Seated around the rustic bar and old-fashioned wooden tables and chairs you will find a late-night crowd, stopping in for a light snack, a special brew, or a quick game of shuffleboard. Shuffleboard? Absolutely! And of course darts, TV, and a jukebox.

Above the bar you will find the chalkboard menu and wine list. The pub offers a light menu featuring homemade soups, chili, nachos, peerless sandwiches, and the salad "o' the day"—even hand-tossed pizza after 6:00 P.M. Providing a friendly atmosphere, the Martin family is quite adept at making their patrons feel at home and "special." They even roast their own pumpkin seeds. Twenty Tank was opened in September of 1990 in an old sheet metal shop by brothers John and Reid Martin. They had had earlier successes at Triple Rock Brewing in nearby Berkeley and Big Time Brewing in Seattle, Washington—both near major university campuses. Breaking the tradition of campus brewpubs, Twenty Tank is nestled in the trendy South of Market area of San Francisco, providing an exciting complement to local hot spots such as the Paradise Lounge, the Oasis, DNA, and Slims.

THE BREWS

Brewer Chris Sheehan with assistants Dave Banas and Jacek Yarrington make a wide variety of flavorful and well-made ales. Selections can vary from as few as three beers on tap to as many as ten, depending on demand and the brewing schedule. They are brewing with a JV Northwest fourteen-barrel system. About fifteen hundred barrels were produced in 1994.

Pellet hops are usually used in the boil and most batches are run through a hop back using whole leaf hops, including Cascade, Cluster, Willamette, and Tettnang. In addition, some of the brews are dry hopped. The wheat beers and darker beers are unfiltered; the lighter styles filtered. There are two beer engines at the bar for serving cask-conditioned ales, usually on Wednesday and Thursday. Servings range from a half pint ($2.00) to a pint ($2.75) and a sixty-ounce pitcher ($9.50). I found the Twenty Tank beers to be nicely balanced, fresh, and very drinkable.

Kinnikinick Club Ale (1.048) in a keg is dark amber, very smooth, and drinkable with a nice fresh hops finish. The cask-conditioned Kinnikinick is a little more complex, maltier, and with a smooth mouth feel. Incidentally, the word "Kinnikinick" comes from a native American word for an herb or a blend of tobacco and herbs. Martin's Mellow Glow Pale Ale (1.049) is a bright pale gold with a light body and flavor and a fresh hoppy finish. The Jack o' Lantern (seasonal) has a deep, orange color with a delicious fresh and fruity aroma and complex malt palate with a hoppy bitter finish. Red Top Ale (1.060) is a simpler brew with deeply roasted malts and fresh hops to balance—it is tasty and very drinkable. Pollywanna Porter (1.068) is black with a deep ruby glow, a coffee aroma, and a rich and complex palate with sweet chocolate, coffee, and roasted malt flavors. Other beers include King Tut Golden Ale (1.054), Moody's High Top Ale (1.076), Bowser's Brown (1.064), Kinnikinick Old Scout Stout (1.080), Nyack Barley Wine (1.080), and Holstein Heferweizen (1.060, unfiltered, made with 40 per cent malted wheat).

Gordon Biersch Brewery Restaurant
33 East San Fernando Street, San Jose, 95113

Telephone: (408) 294-6785; fax, 294-4052
Directions: Between First and Second in downtown San Jose
Hours: Sun–Wed: 11 a.m.–11 p.m.; Thur: till midnight; Fri–Sat: till 1 a.m.
Wheelchair access: Yes
Smoking: No smoking indoors
Entertainment: Live music in the courtyard six nights a week, weather permitting
Tours: On request; advance warning is appreciated
Credit cards: Amex, Diners Club, MasterCard, Visa

I was going open with the words to a song that was popular when we were young and had more hair and smaller waistlines, but thought better of it. Anyway, if you do know the way to San Jose, don't even think of missing Gordon Biersch Brewery Restaurant!

Right across from the Convention Center downtown, in the old Biers Brassiere Brewery building, Gordon Biersch is in the alley between First and Second Streets, through a wrought-iron archway that opens into a tree-lined brick courtyard. The large patio cafe sports old brick walls, flags, umbrella tables, and heat lamps for cool days. Live jazz is provided April through October.

The interior is big, bright and modern, with the tanks soaring through two stories. The loft seats about forty-five and offers a wonderful view of the lower dining area, the seven-barrel brewery, and an exhibition view of the cooking area. The walls display works by local artists in a continually changing gallery, and, yes, they can be purchased.

Head chef Dave Anderson offers an international eclectic menu which is similar to the other Gordon Biersch restaurants. For a full description of the menu, see the Palo Alto entry on page 59. The food here is of the same high quality, featuring such intriguing combinations as Bavarian plate—pork loin, garlic, sausage, prosciutto, goat cheese, and brie. There is a wild mushroom pizza, kung pao prawns, and mahi mahi with pancetta. If you aren't really hungry, or on a smaller budget, the appetizers are enough to satisfy any snack attack.

The atmosphere is comfortable, unpretentious gourmet dining. The servers are truly up with the times, wearing beepers to alert them that their orders are ready. There is always a lively crowd. This popular hotspot in downtown San Jose is not to be missed, but you might want to make reservations. The only time it isn't crowded is when they're closed.

THE BREWS

Masterbrewer Dan Gordon, with the assistance of masterbrewer Tom Davis, supervises the brewing operations at all five of the Gordon Biersch breweries. Richard Johnson is head brewer at San Jose. Richard apprenticed at this location shortly after it opened in 1990. He brewed at the Whistler Brewing Co. in British Columbia for two years and then returned to San Jose. He has been head brewer at Gordon Biersch since 1994.

Richard brews with a seven-barrel, JV Northwest system, which had been installed for the first brewpub at this location, Biers Brasserie. The mash for the specialty brews is done in the traditional German decoction manner. After primary fermentation, each batch is racked to a second tank for cold conditioning. There are seven thirty-barrel lagering tanks. A combination of American, German, Canadian, and English malts are used, depending on the style. Authentic German Hallertau Hersbrucker hops are used. In 1994 the brewery produced twenty-one hundred barrels.

Three beers are on tap at all times—Export, Märzen, and one rotating beer. The rotationals include an unfiltered Dunkles, an unfiltered Doppelbock around Christmas, and a Maibock in the spring. The Export, Märzen, and Dunkles are served in ten-ounce ($2.00) and half-liter glasses ($3.50). Specialty beers are slightly more expensive. Kegs are available for take out in 2.5-, 5-, and 15.5-gallon kegs—please call ahead to reserve one.

As at the other Gordon Biersch Brewery Restaurants, a monthly Brewers Lunch is offered here. It includes an intensive tour of the brewery and lunch with the brewer, and it's held the second Saturday of each month. It costs $25 and reservations as far in advance as possible are recommended.

Tied House Cafe & Brewery

65 North San Pedro Street, San Jose, 95110

TELEPHONE: (408) 295-BREW

DIRECTIONS: FROM I-280, TAKE THE HWY 87 EXIT (GUADALUPE PARKWAY) GOING NORTH, THEN TURN RIGHT ON JAMES STREET, AND RIGHT AGAIN ON SAN PEDRO. IT'S IN DOWNTOWN SAN JOSE ON SAN PEDRO SQUARE, THREE BLOCKS EAST OF THE SHARKS ARENA

HOURS: DAILY: 11A.M.–MIDNIGHT

WHEELCHAIR ACCESS: YES

SMOKING: ONLY IN DESIGNATED AREAS

ENTERTAINMENT: LIVE MUSIC EVERY FRIDAY AND SATURDAY NIGHT (JAZZ, RHYTHM & BLUES, ETC.), SHUFFLEBOARD, DARTS

TOURS: BY APPOINTMENT

CREDIT CARDS: AMEX, DINERS CLUB, DISCOVER, MASTERCARD, VISA

The Tied House in Mountain View was such a smashing success the parent company, the Redwood Coast Brewing Co., decided to do it again. It opened on downtown's San Pedro Square in August 1991, making it San Jose's fourth brewpub (though two have since closed). After the San Jose Tied House opened, it was followed by a third in Alameda in December of the same year.

The San Jose facility is every bit as long as the original is square, stretching the entire width of a city block. It looks like it could accommodate two bowling alleys placed end to end. The interior is awesome, with seating for 650, counting the beer garden. Behind the cream-colored stucco front with red-trimmed windows is a long oak bar under beamed cathedral ceilings and hundreds of skylights. Gleaming stainless-steel fermenters and serving tanks can be seen through large windows behind the bar. The copper-clad brewhouse is just past the bar on the left. This spectacular view of the brewery is enough to make a beer lover's heart throb.

The restaurant seems to continue forever until reaching the trellised beer garden in the back. On the right, bare brick walls are accented with framed examples of modern art and natural wood trim. Wooden booths line the walls, and tables are set with plain white or checkered tablecloths. Dozens of ferns hang from the beams (the observant will note that they are fake). A large display kitchen runs along the left side of the room.

San Jose residents flock to the Tied House, and if you want to avoid the noisy, boisterous atmosphere, try the beer garden—its trellises drip with trumpet vines, announcing a more intimate and laid-back atmosphere.

The restaurant offers the same ample menu as the other Tied Houses, featuring many items that are either prepared with beer or that complement the beers. They specialize in appetizers, including oysters Rockefeller and panko calamari. Soups, sandwiches, and the famous Tied Burger are offered, as well as such entrees as applewood-smoked baby back ribs, pasta, seafood, house-made sausages, and Louisiana blackened catfish.

The Tied House and Gordon Biersch Brewery in downtown San Jose are within walking distance of each other. While you're in the neighborhood, check out the Peralta Adobe (the oldest building in San Jose), St. Joseph's Catholic Church, the Center for Performing Arts, or stroll around the San Jose State University campus.

THE BREWS

Tied House beers are very gentle beers, and they have taken many awards at the GABF in Denver. The beers are made with a twenty-barrel system made in Oregon by JV Northwest. All the beers are filtered, except for the wheat beers. Production has increased steadily since opening. By 1994 it had reached three thousand barrels.

Chris Ewing is head of the brewing operations. Ewing had brewed at San Francisco Brewing before coming to the Tied House, where he was trained under the tutelage of the late Cheuck Toms, the original Tied House brewmaster.

Normally, eight beers are on tap at all times. Offerings change from time to time, but a fairly complete list would include the following: Tied House Amber Light (1.032, lightly malty), Alpine Pearl Pale (1.055), Berliner Weisse Ginger, Amber Ale (1.048), Peach Amber (a tasty fruit beer with a nice balance between the peach and the malt), Ironwood Dark (1.048, medium dark with a little hop crispness in the finish), Passion Pale (1.048, made with passion fruit extract), Light Dark, Tied House Porter (a delectable brew with notes of bittersweet chocolate), Oktoberfest/Märzen (a fruity version), and Yule Tied.

LIND BREWING CO.
1933 Davis (Westgate Mall #177), San Leandro, 94577

TELEPHONE: (510) 562-0866
DIRECTIONS: FROM I-880, TAKE THE DAVIS STREET WEST EXIT; IT'S LOCATED IN THE WESTGATE MALL, BEHIND COSTCO
TOURS: FRI 4–6P.M.

Roger Lind, president and brewmaster at Lind Brewing, likes loud music and thinks the yeast does, too. He plays rock 'n roll, reggae, blues, and the Grateful Dead loud enough to keep the yeast cells wide awake and doing their thing. Any yeast cells that like Schubert or Mozart will find no inspiration here.

Lind Brewing is an unusual brewery. It started small, has stayed small, and if Roger has his way, it will never get very big. Roger is a native of Berkeley who began brewing at home in 1981. When brewpubs began opening in the Bay Area, he decided that one day he would open his own. His first job in the industry came in 1986 at Triple Rock. Within six months he moved on to brew at the Devil Mountain Brewery in Walnut Creek. In 1988 he became brewmaster at the ill-fated Golden Gate Brewery in San Francisco.

When Golden Gate closed, Roger decided it was time to open his own brewpub. However, he did not have the capital to go it alone, and he did not want to bring in partners who would have a say in how the operations were run. So Roger decided to open a small craft brewery. He found an empty Caterpillar warehouse in San Leandro and rehabbed it for a brewery. His first beers were distributed in September 1989. Lind Brewing is the only brewery in the Bay Area that packages exclusively in kegs. They are available in fifteen-gallon or five-liter sizes and need to be ordered a few days in advance.

THE BREWS

Roger and assistants Mike Manty and Mike Bancroft are brewing with a fourteen-barrel brew kettle manufactured by JV Northwest. He started with a fourteen-barrel primary fermenter and eight converted Grundies for conditioning tanks. The mash tun and hot liquor tank are converted dairy tanks. Four fourteen-barrel unitanks and a fourteen-barrel bright beer tank were added later.

The beers are made with domestic, two-row pale malt and specialty malts, with the exception of English caramel malt in the Drake's Ale. A great variety of pelletized hops are used, all domestic, except for Czech Saaz and English Goldings. Drake's Ale and Drake's Gold are dry hopped.

Most of the beers are filtered—the Drake's Stout and a few specialty beers are not. Roger makes a few cask-conditioned beers for special customers. Production in 1994 just topped a thousand barrels.

Drake's Gold, Drake's Ale, and Sir Francis Stout are available year round. The rest are seasonal. Drake's Gold (1.052) is very smooth and crisp, with a hoppy aroma and flavor, but not very bitter (bronze 1990 GABF) made with 20 percent wheat malt, dry hopped with Cascades and Hallertau. The Drake's Ale has a copper color and a complex malty palate with an accent on the hops. The Sir Francis Stout (1.064) is very roasty with notes of coffee and chocolate. The cask-conditioned Bitter Ale is fresh and fruity with roasted malts and a well-balanced, hoppy, bitter finish.

Lind Raspberry Wheat (1.045), available in the summer, is made with 30 percent wheat malt and hopped with Cascades—it tastes like raspberry-flavored light ale. Lind Autumn Fest has a reddish-copper color with a nice, tall, creamy, off-white head. It is complex, with a sweet and fruity entry, caramelized malt in the middle, and quite a bit of fresh hops in the finish—a very drinkable and satisfying brew. Drake's Brown Ale (1.048), available in the winter, has a beautiful copper color and a sweet, hoppy tanginess with lots of deeply roasted malt. Bacchus Ale is very big and malty with a pronounced Hallertau finish (6.6 percent alcohol by weight). Drake's Nog (for the Christmas season) is made from the same recipe as the Brown Ale with the addition of cinnamon, cardamom, and other spices. A second Christmas beer is Jolly Roger's Holiday Ale (9 percent alcohol), with an intense, rich flavor.

Barley & Hops Brewery, Blues Club & Smokehouse

201 South B Street, San Mateo, 94401

Telephone: Restaurant, (415) 348-7808; Brewery, 348-4889; Fax, 348-8789
Directions: From Hwy 101, take the 3rd Avenue exit, then right on B; it's at the corner of B Street and 2nd Avenue
Hours: Daily 11a.m.–1a.m.
Wheelchair access: Yes
Smoking: Upstairs
Entertainment: Live blues bands Wed–Sun, TV, Pool
Tours: Appointments preferred
Credit cards: Amex, Diners Club, MasterCard, Visa, JCB

Brewpubs in San Mateo County were a long time coming, but they finally arrived in the spring of 1995 with a vengeance. With a population of over five hundred thousand one would have thought someone would have opened a brewpub before then. Burlingame Station opened in March, and on April 8, only a few weeks later, the Barley & Hops opened in San Mateo.

Owner Aaron Ferer, who also owns several successful restaurants on the peninsula, has refurbished the historic Merkel Building and put new life in the old girl. A San Mateo landmark since 1931, the Merkel Building is classic Art Deco with a towered facade, large arched windows, and a glazed terra-cotta finish.

Inside, the Barley & Hops is really three brewpubs in one. As you enter, you find yourself in the main dining room with a very high ceiling, wood tones, and a dark green and burgundy color scheme. It has its own wooden bar and a display kitchen. The brewery can be seen both from the dining area and the bar. A gaming parlor and atrium dining are located on the second floor. The gaming parlor is a beer-lover's playpen, featuring its own bar, four pool tables, shuffleboard, darts, big-screen TV, a fireplace, and a humidor for cigar smokers. If you are into music, head down to the basement to the 130-seat Blues Club, with a bar and dance floor. The Blues Club is currently bringing in top acts from Chicago. There is also valet parking ($2.00).

The cuisine has a Texas smokehouse theme with many barbecue items, prime steaks, Chicago deep-dish pizza, fresh fish, appetizers, soups, and salads.

THE BREWS

The beers are made by brewmaster R. J. Trent, who was brewmaster at Riptide's in San Diego before coming to the Barley & Hops. R. J. is using a fourteen-barrel system manufactured by the Pub. The beers are made with two-row American pale malts, British specialty malts, domestic pellet hops, and Saaz hops from the Czech Republic. A few of the beers are dry hopped with leaf hops.

Four to six beers are usually on tap, four or five of which are regulars. Two of the beers are filtered—Golden Pale Ale (1.056) and Roaring Red (1.060). Three are unfiltered—RyePA (1.068), Oatmeal Stout (1.076), and Raspberry Wheat (1.056).

The beers are served in eleven- ($2.25), sixteen- ($3.00), and twenty-one-ounce glasses ($4.00). Four-ounce samplers are available for $1.00. Beer is available for take out and can be delivered within the local area.

PACIFIC TAP & GRILL
812 4th Street, San Rafael, 94901

TELEPHONE: (415) 457-9711; FAX, 457-2299
DIRECTIONS: FROM HWY 101, TAKE THE SAN RAFAEL EXIT, GO WEST ON THIRD STREET AND THEN TURN RIGHT ON LINCOLN. IT'S IN DOWNTOWN SAN RAFAEL ON THE CORNER OF 4TH AND LINCOLN
HOURS: MON–THUR: 11:30A.M.–10P.M.; FRI–SAT: TILL 11P.M.; SUN: 12:30P.M.–9:30P.M.
WHEELCHAIR ACCESS: YES
SMOKING: NO SMOKING INDOORS
ENTERTAINMENT: LIVE MUSIC ON OCCASION
TOURS: BY APPOINTMENT
CREDIT CARDS: AMEX, MASTERCARD, VISA

The next time you're on Hwy 101 whizzing by the San Rafael exit, slow down and make a stop at the Pacific Tap & Grill. Here will be found not only some delectable brews but outstanding victuals as well.

When the restaurant brewery opened in 1993, chef Eric Lenard had been dubbed one of the rising culinary stars of northern California. Although Lenard moved on to greener pastures and has been ably replaced by Benito Malivert, his influence can still be felt in the menu. Not content to play second fiddle to the chef, head brewer Drew Goldberg has already won a gold medal at the GABF.

The facade is a rather plain stucco with green awnings, under which picture windows provide customers with a view of downtown San Rafael. Inside the arched doorway is a pleasant restaurant with a high, unfinished wood, barrel-vaulted ceiling and red brick walls with Roman columns. The handsome, copper-clad brewhouse and stainless-steel fermenters sit enclosed in glass along the left side of the restaurant. Out the back door is the beer garden with seating for seventy. The garden has a red tiled floor and a hard, removable roof. Heaters are provided for cooler weather.

The lunchtime crowd is very big at Pacific Tap, with shoppers and office workers coming in for a brew and a bite to eat. The menu offers many appetizers, including buffalo wings, chicken satay, and a very popular item, barbecued oysters on the half shell. There are six different salads—the caesar salad has developed a devoted following. There are many sandwiches as well, pastas, and several grilled and smoked items. These include coriander grilled pork chops, rum-soaked shrimp with mango relish, and baby back ribs house-smoked over oak and mesquite. California wines and desserts are also available.

Pacific Tap & Grill is owned by Bob Keller (who was involved in the opening of Los Gatos Brewing), Keith Borral, Jr., and Keith Borral, Sr. They hope to open many more brewpubs in northern California in the coming years.

THE BREWS
Brewer Drew Goldberg has Mission Gold and Bootjack Amber on tap at all times. Mission Gold (1.044) is a filtered American pale ale with a tangy-hoppy finish and maltiness to balance. Bootjack Amber (1.045) has a more subtle, roasted malty character. Two seasonal beers are on tap as well. On my visit I tried Noah's Dark (1.047), which took the silver medal in the porter category at the Great American Beer Festival. It was well balanced with a complex roasted-malt character. Unfiltered and medium brown in color, its signature comes from Vienna and dark Munich malts. I found it pleasant and immensely drinkable. The last beer sampled was Brewberry Ale (1.042). It was hazy and had a fruity-floral aroma and blueberry palate. Other beers include High Time Barleywine (1.088), Scottish Ale (1.068), and various wheat beers.

Drew happened into brewing several years ago while looking through the yellow pages. He was looking to buy a keg of some good imported beer when he came across the heading "beer and beermaking supplies." By the end of the day he had visited a homebrew supply shop and made his first purchase of beermaking equipment and ingredients. This eventually led to a masters in brewing science and engineering from the University of California at Davis. Drew has also passed the associate membership exam of the highly regarded Institute of Brewing in London.

Drew and his assistant brew with a fourteen-barrel system manufactured by JV Northwest. The fermenters and serving tanks are seven barrels in size, requiring the batches to be split. Drew uses a great variety of malts, which are milled in house, and employs mostly American pellet hops. The lighter beers are filtered; the darker, specialty beers are usually unfiltered. In 1994, they produced 850 barrels.

Normally, four to five beers are on tap. A set of samplers costs $3.00. Twelve-ounce servings cost $3.00 and pints $3.25. Beer is available for take out in gallon containers.

FAULTLINE BREWING
1235 Oakmead Parkway, Sunnyvale, 94086

TELEPHONE: (408) 736-BREW; FAX, 736-2752
DIRECTIONS: FROM HWY 101, TAKE LAWRENCE EXPRESSWAY SOUTH EXIT, TURN LEFT ON OAKMEAD; IT IS ON THE CORNER OF OAKMEAD AND LAKESIDE
HOURS: DAILY: 11:30A.M.–CLOSING (APPROXIMATELY 2A.M.)
WHEELCHAIR ACCESS: YES
SMOKING: NO SMOKING INDOORS
TOURS: BY APPOINTMENT
CREDIT CARDS: AMEX, DINERS CLUB, MASTERCARD, VISA

Sunnyvale's second brewpub opened on December 2, 1994. In contrast to the downtown setting of Stoddard's, Faultline Brewing offers a lovely beer garden in a bucolic, lakeside setting—what a great place to take time out from the Bay Area rat race. And since it's sitting on top of the San Andreas Fault, what's a more natural name than "Faultline"? Leave it to Californians to make light of their constantly life-threatening situation. Hey, if you can't beat 'em, join 'em.

Inside the modern gray wood exterior is an open and airy multileveled restaurant with modern lines. The lounge bar features two fifty-foot, black granite bars. The entire brewing operation is displayed behind glass behind the main bar. In the middle of the restaurant is a large, elevated dining area offering views of both the lounge bar and brewery and the lake. Beyond this is another, lower-level dining area offering views of the lake and the beer garden through plate-glass windows. The restaurant has a high-tech industrial feel with open wood-beam ceilings, lots of corrugated metal and stainless steel, and a maroon-and-black color theme.

This is not one of those "pub-grub" kinds of places, but rather, it offers fine dining on tables draped in white linen. General partner Mark Perry says they do a big lunch trade and have substantially different menus for lunch and dinner. For the lunch crowd they offer some splendid appetizers, such as grilled beef satay, oysters on the half shell, steamed New Zealand cockles, and house-made focaccia topped with pesto, sundried tomatoes, artichoke hearts, arugula, and asiago cheese. These are followed by a choice of seven different salads, ten different gourmet sandwiches, and four different pasta dishes. Entrees include grilled marinated chicken paillard, grilled cumin-rubbed pork, grilled vegetable lasagna, shrimp etouffee, and roasted short ribs.

And that's just lunch. Dinner appetizers include many of the lunch ones plus stuffed Portobello mushroom, tempura ahi rolls, and baked brie. The imaginative dinner salads include spring duck salad and warm apple and potato. The pastas are the same as lunch, but when you turn to the entrees, you are in for more surprises—pan-seared salmon medallions, grilled applewood-smoked pork loin, grilled vegetable napoleon, and roasted Maple Leaf duck, just to name a few. They also offer a children's menu and a substantial wine list.

THE BREWS

Greg Friday, a University of California at Davis graduate, does the brewing honors at Faultline. He brews on a twenty-barrel system, keeping three regulars and three specialty beers on tap at all times. The regulars include Golden Ale, which is smooth and light with a fresh, hoppy aroma and palate (it is dry hopped); Pale, which offers a little more heft in the bitterness department; and Stout, which is dry and smooth with a creamy body. The regulars are filtered; the specials may or may not be filtered, depending on the style. The first two specialty beers on deck were Hefeweizen and Scotch Ale. Greg also makes his own root beer.

Beers are available in twelve-ounce ($2.25) and pint glasses ($3.25). Sets of three six-ounce samplers sell for $4.25.

Stoddard's Brewhouse & Eatery & Benchmark Brewery

111 South Murphy Avenue (P.O. Box 70128), Sunnyvale, 94086

TELEPHONE: (408) 733-7824; FAX, 733-8969

DIRECTIONS: From Hwy 82—El Camino Real—turn on Mathilda Avenue going north. Pass Sunnyvale Town Shopping Center on your right; take a right on Washington Avenue and left on Murphy

HOURS: Mon–Fri: 11:30a.m.–1a.m.; Sat–Sun: noon–1a.m.

WHEELCHAIR ACCESS: Yes

SMOKING: None

ENTERTAINMENT: Live music, TV

TOURS: Drop-in; appointments preferred

CREDIT CARDS: Amex, Discover, Mastercard, Visa

In the midst of all the hubbub of Silicon Valley lies an oasis in the city of Sunnyvale. Located in the Old Town section of Murphy Station, Stoddard's Brewhouse and Eatery gives the impression of a cool, restful atmosphere. Residing on quaint, tree-lined Murphy Avenue, the pastel yellow and blue exterior draws you to the elegant interior. As you walk inside, the open staircase accented with black railings in the center of the main dining area draws your eyes upward to the balcony, providing an open, airy ambience. Track lighting accents the sponge-painted walls. The skylight above the stairs brings light into the cool interior, while the street-level windows add to the fresh, open feeling. It's like being outdoors, without the heat and traffic.

A spacious lobby separates the brewery and bar from the exhibition-style kitchen with its grill framed in hardwood and its oak-fueled oven. The fermentation and serving tanks are displayed behind the bar in a glass-walled brewing room. The dining area provides ample seating with cloth-covered tables and fresh flowers, all of which complement the excellent menu. Reservations are recommended for dinner.

For starters, you might want to visit Stoddard's with a group of friends, so you can order more of the tempting dishes and share! The appetizers alone are worth the visit: crispy flatbread made from hummus, eggplant, and whipped feta; brewhouse baked oysters with spinach, feta, and lemon; or Tabasco strings—Louisiana fried onions. They offer a salad for every taste, from the simple but delicious house romaine to the smoked salmon, citrus spinach, or Mediterranean chicken salad.

Entrees include mesquite-grilled pork chops, Pilarcitos seafood stew (with mussels, shrimp, clams, and fresh fish), and baby back ribs with a choice of Lone Star Dry Seasoned or Stoddard's Barbecue Brew. Or you could just go straight for the pizza. Their Italian sausage pizza is for traditional pizza-lovers while the smoked salmon and the pesto pizzas send you California dreamin'. But you can't leave without trying one of their delicious pastas: bow tie pasta with broccoli, peas, and cream sauce, or potato gnocchi with fennel sausage and chicken, Pomodoro cream sauce, and Mascarpone cheese. Stoddard's also offers daily specials.

Whether you decide to try a little of everything or keep returning until your curiosity is satisfied, you will leave Stoddard's feeling as though you have been someplace special. Reservations are recommended for dinner.

THE BREWS

The beers at Stoddard's are made by brewmaster/owner Bob Stoddard with the assistance of head brewer Michael Gray. Bob Stoddard entered the craft brewing business from the marketing end. In 1985 he was working for the sales and marketing department of Miller Brewing Co. when he discovered the Palo Alto Brewing Co., one of the early California craft breweries. At that time they were selling cask-conditioned ales to bars and restaurants. Bob became fascinated with craft brewing and went to work for Palo Alto, marketing their beers. Learning that the brewery was in danger of going broke, he soon took over the brewing operations. Shortly after, Palo Alto began brewing Pete's Wicked Ale under contract. In 1987 the brewery closed and Pete's was soon being made in the Midwest. The brewing equipment was sold to the Tied House in Mountain View and Bob became involved in the start of that brewery. While at the Tied House, Bob began putting together the plan for opening his own brewpub. He finally did so, in April of 1993.

The beers at Stoddard's are the product of Bob's increasing interest in brewing authentic-tasting beers. The custom-made, JV Northwest twenty-barrel brewhouse and the rest of the operation reflect Bob's familiarity with brewing. He made sure it was very easy to use and clean.

The beers are made from a base of two-row American pale malt to which is added specialty malts from England. The malts are milled in house. For hops, they used a combination of domestic and imported pellets for bittering, flavoring, and aroma, and fresh, leaf Cascades to dry hop the Pale Ale and the ESB. All of the beers are filtered. In 1994, fifteen hundred barrels were produced.

Beers are available in sampler ($1.00), half-pint ($1.90), pint ($3.00), and pitcher ($11.00) servings. Normally three regular—Kölsch, Pale Ale, and Porter—and one rotational beer are on tap. Take-out beer is available in half kegs, kegs, and half-gallon jars.

The Kölsch (1.054) is bright gold with a light, fruity aroma and a delicate, yet complex, malty palate with a fairly long hoppy-bitter finish. The Pale Ale (1.050) is amber with a smooth, roasted malt palate. The ESB (1.053) is dark copper and has a rich, malty palate balanced by tasty, fruity-tangy notes and a bitter finish. The Porter (1.056) is a beautiful reddish auburn and has a rich, deeply-roasted malt palate. Kristall Weizen (1.052), is made with 65 percent malted wheat. In 1994 the ESB took a bronze at the Great American Beer Festival.

BLACK DIAMOND BREWING CO.

2330 North Main Street, Walnut Creek, 94596

TELEPHONE: (510) 943-2330
DIRECTIONS: FROM HWY 680, TAKE THE NORTH MAIN STREET EXIT. IF YOU'RE COMING FROM THE SOUTH, TURN LEFT ON NORTH MAIN; IF YOU'RE COMING FROM THE NORTH, TURN RIGHT. AT THE FIRST MAJOR INTERSECTION, TURN LEFT. BLACK DIAMOND IS RIGHT ON THE CORNER OF NORTH MAIN AND PARKSIDE, ACROSS FROM THE MARRIOTT HOTEL AND THREE BLOCKS NORTH OF THE WALNUT CREEK BART STATION
HOURS: SUN–THUR: 11A.M.–MIDNIGHT; FRI–SAT: TILL 1A.M.
WHEELCHAIR ACCESS: YES
SMOKING: NONE
ENTERTAINMENT: LIVE MUSIC ON SUN
TOURS: BY APPOINTMENT
CREDIT CARDS: AMEX, MASTERCARD, VISA

It would be appropriate to call Black Diamond "the Cadillac of restaurant breweries"—if only because it is housed in a building designed to be an auto dealership. Opening in February 1995, it is one of the newest entries in the field and the first brewpub to operate in Walnut Creek since the brewery was removed from the Devil Mountain Brewery Restaurant & Pub in the old railway station in 1990. Black Diamond is as sleek and flashy as Devil Mountain was old-fashioned and sedate. Behind the curved, twelve-foot-high plate-glass widows is a split-level restaurant connected by a spiral staircase, with seating for 165, along with ample room in the bar. Behind the bar stands the entire stainless-steel brewery, gleaming under track lighting. The interior is highlighted with warm mahogany woods and splashes of color.

All of the items served at Black Diamond are prepared from scratch in the display kitchen on the main floor. The menu combines its six craft beers with regional American bistro fare, including cheddar beer soup with broccoli, Weizen-battered onion rings, an ale-steamed corned beef reuben sandwich, a blackened chicken breast lagniappe sandwich and sauteed Angus filet mignon with India Pale-infused shallot sauce. Also offered are a variety of rich and flavorful desserts, including the Black Diamond chocolate brownie and the caramelized apple cheesecake, and a substantial wine list. There is free valet parking for dinner only from Tuesday to Saturday.

THE BREWS

Brewmaster and general manager Darren Whitcher had been homebrewing for nine years with the idea of one day opening his own brewery. He combined his interests and talents with co-owners Joseph Garaventa and Timothy Bredbenner. His new "homebrew" set-up features a fifteen-barrel brewhouse, two thirty-barrel fermenters, four fifteen-barrel fermenters and eight serving tanks manufactured by Liquid Assets, Inc. Regular beers include Black Diamond Weizen, a traditional Bavarian wheat beer; Black Diamond Premium, a golden ale; Aftershock Pale Ale, with a long, hoppy finish; Steep Trail Amber Ale, cask-conditioned; and Blackjack Stout. The first seasonal beer out of the serving tanks was Winter Strong Ale.

The wait staff has been well trained in the art of serving specialty beers, and each style of beer is served in a distinctive glass. Beers are available in .2-liter ($1.75) and .4-liter servings ($3.00). One-liter samplers are available for $1.00 each, or a set of six for $5.00. Pitchers cost $10.00.

Central Coast and Valleys

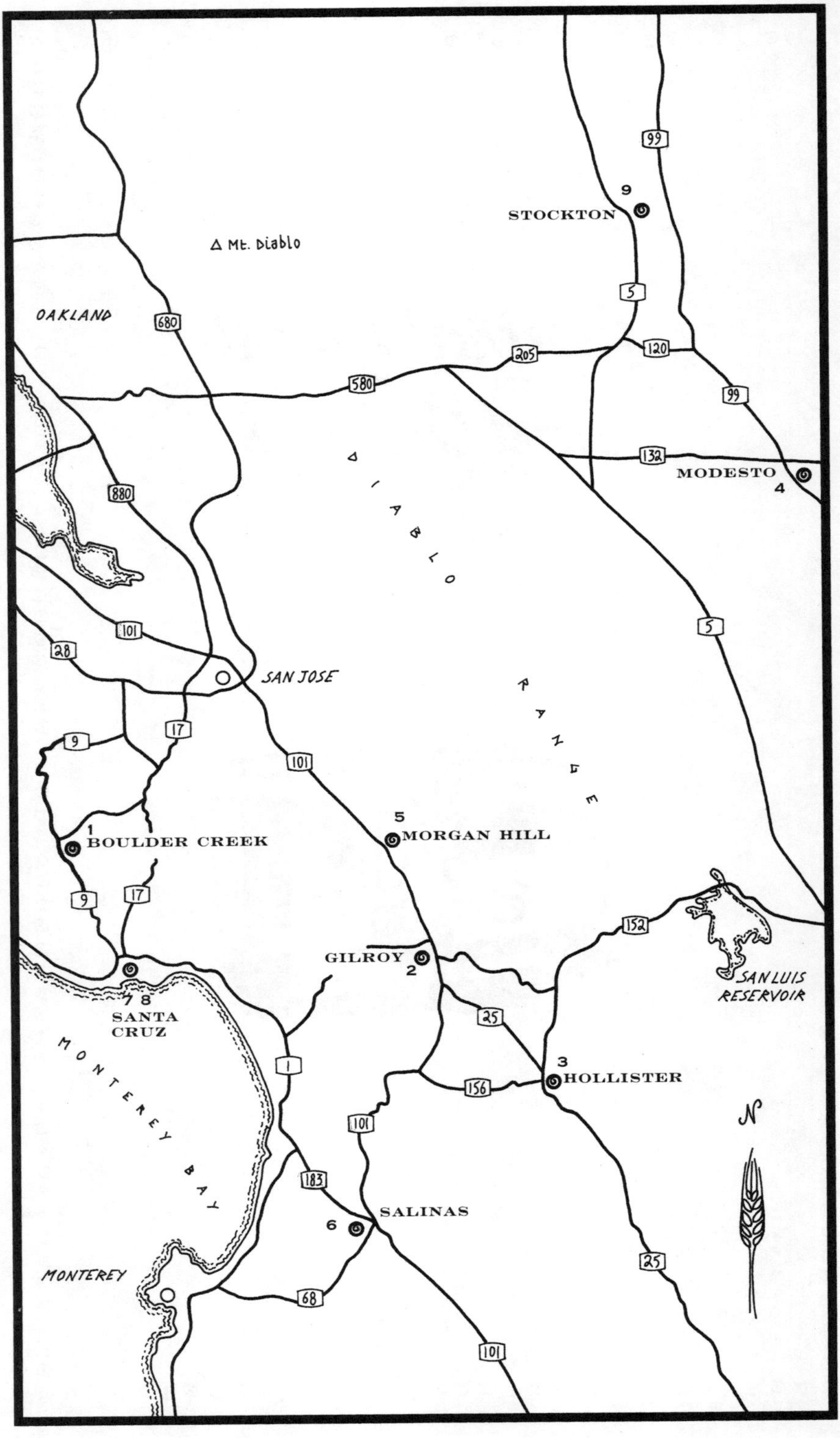
99
9
STOCKTON
Δ Mt. Diablo
5
OAKLAND
680
205
120
580
99
132
MODESTO
4
880
DIABLO RANGE
101
5
28
SAN JOSE
17
9
101
5
MORGAN HILL
1
BOULDER CREEK
9
17
152
GILROY
2
SAN LUIS RESERVOIR
7 8
SANTA CRUZ
25
MONTEREY BAY
1
3
HOLLISTER
156
N
101
183
SALINAS
6
25
MONTEREY
68
101

CENTRAL COAST AND VALLEYS

CITY	BREWERY (MAP KEY)	PAGE
BOULDER CREEK	BOULDER CREEK BREWING CO. & BOULDER CREEK GRILL & CAFE (1)	90
GILROY	COAST RANGE BREWING CO. (2)	92
HOLLISTER	SAN ANDREAS BREWING CO. (3)	93
MODESTO	ST. STAN'S BREWERY & RESTAURANT (4)	95
MORGAN HILL	EL TORO BREWING CO. (5)	97
SALINAS	CARMEL BREWING CO. (6)	98
SANTA CRUZ	SANTA CRUZ BREWING CO. & FRONT STREET PUB (7)	99
	SEABRIGHT BREWERY PUB & RESTAURANT (8)	101
STOCKTON	EL DORADO BREWING CO. (9)	103

Boulder Creek Brewing Co. & Boulder Creek Grill & Cafe

13040 Highway 9, Boulder Creek, 95006

TELEPHONE: (408) 338-7882
DIRECTIONS: It's in the center of town on the east side of Hwy 9
HOURS: Sun.–Thur.: Noon–11 p.m.; Fri–Sat: till midnight
WHEELCHAIR ACCESS: Yes
SMOKING: Only in designated areas
ENTERTAINMENT: Occasional live music
TOURS: By appointment
CREDIT CARDS: Amex, MasterCard, Visa

One of the most beautiful drives in California is along Highway 1, through the central coast region. There you will find beaches, enchanting views from sea cliffs, and lighthouses here and there. As you wind your way along the coast into the redwood forests, do yourself a favor and take a short detour at Highway 9. A dozen steep and winding miles will bring you to Boulder Creek, a charming old logging town nestled in the Santa Cruz Mountains. Near Big Basin State Park, the area boasts more than eighteen thousand acres of redwoods.

Boulder Creek Brewing was first opened in 1990 by locals Steve Wyman and Nancy Long. It resides in the old post office located on the main street. It has a "storefront" entrance shaded by awnings that lead to a rustic interior, featuring hardwood floors and paneling, a light oak bar with antique soda tap handles and beer taps, old-fashioned globe lamps suspended from the ceiling, and a skylight. You can sit at the bar and watch the brewers at work, or go next door to the dining room. The brewers also work behind the bar and share their enthusiasm and knowledge about their beer—tours of the brewery and samples of the beers are available.

Originally a grocery store, the dining room is separated from the bar by an oak partition with etched glass inserts. Choose one of the antique tables, pull up an old wooden chair, and relax under the gentle breeze of the ceiling fans while perusing the menu. Appetizers offered are Thai-style sweet potatoes, garlic fries, onion rings, and nachos. There is a full menu ranging from sandwiches and burgers—with or without meat—to a full dinner. You can feast on London broil, pasta dishes, and chicken California-style. There is even a good kids' menu. In addition to the many styles and varieties of handcrafted beer, they offer raspberry iced tea, sodas, assorted hot teas, coffees and—to complement their exquisite dessert menu—French roast coffee.

After your meal you might want to wander to the back room where there is a pool table and a smaller bar. It's worth the trip just to view the Victorian spider-web wooden frame in front of the bar.

THE BREWS

Head brewer Peter Catizone and brewer Steve Hanecak make only one beer on a regular basis: Redwood Ale. All the rest rotate at Peter's whim, something that brings customers back to try out his latest invention. Before becoming head brewer, Peter homebrewed and did a stint as bartender and assistant brewer. He brews on a locally made, six-barrel system. Peter uses primarily British ingredients, including the malts, hops, and yeast. He is particularly fond of Hugh Baird malts and Kent Golding hops. Pellet hops are used for bittering, flower hops for flavoring and aroma. The lighter beers are filtered; the heavier ones are not. Production in 1994 was just under four hundred barrels. Beers are available in ten-ounce ($2.25) and sixteen-ounce servings ($2.75) and sixty-ounce pitchers ($8.25). Prices are reduced during happy hour (4:00–6:00 P.M., Mon–Fri). Usually three to four beers are on tap at a time. Quart Mason jars are available for take out.

The Redwood Ale (1.051) is pleasantly malty, fruity with a touch of hops and slightly winy. Lompico Pale Ale, named after the town where Peter lives, is a hazy gold with a hoppy character. Buzz Saw Bock (1.065) is a deep, reddish brown, slightly sweet and malty, but with a very nice hoppy-tangy finish (it is named after a movie starring Matthew Broderick that was filmed in Boulder Creek; originally billed as *Welcome to Buzz Saw*, it was released under the title *Out on a Limb*). Ghost Rail Pale Ale (1.050) is a golden amber with a mild but noticeable British hop character. Other brews include Royal ESB (1.056), Black Bear Ale (1.058, an English porter), Festbier (1.055), Boulder Creek Porter (1.056), and Oatmeal Molasses Stout (1.057).

COAST RANGE BREWING CO.
7050 Monterey Street, Gilroy, 95020

TELEPHONE: (408) 842-1000;
FAX, 842-1025
DIRECTIONS: FROM U.S. 101, TAKE THE 10TH STREET EXIT; GO WEST ON 10TH STREET THREE BLOCKS; RIGHT ON MONTEREY; IT'S IN THE SOUTH END OF DOWNTOWN
TOURS: ON A DROP-IN BASIS; BEST TO CALL FIRST

What do beer and garlic have in common? Nothing, but Gilroy, "the garlic capital of the world," has its very own brewery as of 1995. Owner Ron Erskine was in the construction business and looking for a career change. He was a fan of the new craft beers and decided brewing would be the perfect occupation.

THE BREWS

Brewmaster Peter Licht, fresh out of the University of California at Davis masterbrewers program, is excited to be in the brewing business. After receiving his undergraduate degree in liberal arts from the Columbia University, he moved to California and learned to do something useful: make beer at home. Like Erskine, he enjoyed the new craft beers so much he decided to brew them himself.

Peter is brewing with a twenty-barrel system, manufactured by Liquid Assets, and forty-barrel fermenters. The pale malts are a combination of American and English two-row. Specialty malts are from the United Kingdom. The hops are all American pellet hops. The Desperado is dry hopped. Both of their products are filtered.

Coast Range began distributing its beers in kegs on March 1, 1995. The beers are available from Santa Cruz to the north end of the San Francisco Bay. Their two beers are Desperado Special Bitter (1.054) and Blackberry Wheat (1.046, made with blackberry extract). The beers are distributed in 2.25-gallon party pigs, five-gallon and fifteen-gallon kegs, and half-gallon jugs that are also available at the brewery.

SAN ANDREAS BREWING CO.
737 San Benito Street, Hollister, 95023

TELEPHONE: (408) 637-7074
DIRECTIONS: FOLLOW SAN BENITO STREET, JUST OFF ROUTE 156, WHICH LEADS TO DOWNTOWN
HOURS: SUN, TUES–THUR: 11A.M.–10P.M.; FRI–SAT: 11A.M.–11P.M.
WHEELCHAIR ACCESS: YES
SMOKING: NO SMOKING INDOORS
ENTERTAINMENT: LIVE MUSIC FRI AND SAT, TV, DARTS, SHUFFLEBOARD
CREDIT CARDS: NONE

Located on top of three major fault lines, Hollister is the "earthquake capital" of California. So, if your beer mug begins to shake, don't worry: it's just another—yawn—earthquake.

When the ground-shaking gets a little more violent than usual, the question people usually ask themselves is, "Should I stand in a doorway or go outside?" Well, in Hollister there is no question of where to go—people head to the San Andreas Brewing Company on San Benito Street, due to owner Bill Millar's policy of serving nickel drafts during earthquakes. When the Loma Prieta earthquake struck on October 17, 1989, the brewpub quickly swelled with locals eager to fill up on "cheap beer." So many customers turned out that Bill had to politely ask some folks to leave.

San Andreas is housed in the Baywood Creamery building, dating to 1940, with thick, yellow tile walls. The dining room is homey, with oak floors, beer memorabilia on the walls, a 1950s jukebox, and an antique player piano. The clientele is made up of locals and the occasional beer tourist.

Just off the dining room is a small bar, featuring the original stools from the creamery's dairy bar, an old shuffleboard, darts, and pinball machines.

The menu features fish and chips, calamari, burgers, and light pub fare. In addition to the beer, they make their own bread, potato chips, root beer, and cream soda. The "Earthquake" burger has been dubbed the second-best hamburger in the West by the guidebook *The Best Places in Northern California* edited by Rebecca Poole Forée and Stephanie Irving.

THE BREWS
The beers are made by brewmaster Garrie Bryant, and owner Bill Millar is also actively involved. Bill has a background in wine chemistry and cannery operations; Garrie is a graduate of the brewing school at the University of California at Davis.

The fifteen-barrel brewhouse was manufactured by JV Northwest; the original fermenters were made locally. Two-row domestic malts are used, which are milled at the brewery. American and German-style fresh leaf hops are used. The local water, which is very hard, is not filtered before use. The beers are all filtered, and bottled beers are flash pasteurized. Output in 1994 was 280 barrels.

Beers are available in eight-ounce servings ($1.25), twelve-ounce servings ($1.75), and pints ($2.50). Beer to go is available in twenty-two-ounce bottles, and three-, five-, seven-, and fifteen-gallon kegs. Normally, six beers are on tap at all times.

Earthquake Pale is bright gold with a malty aroma and lots of fresh hops in the palate. It finishes with a delicious, crisp kiss of hops. Aftershock Wheat is made in the true German wheat style with a hazy gold color and a nice, clovy, wheaty aroma and palate. Seismic Ale is deep amber with a malty, sour palate. Kit Fox is bright copper and has a sweet, roasted-malt palate. October Quake 1994 (a German Märzen) has a nice, bright copper look and a sweet, complex malty palate. Earthquake Porter is black with sourish, chocolate-coffee palate. Survivor Stout is jet black with a creamy brown head—there is quite a bit of dry roasted barley and chocolate in the palate, and some notes of licorice as well. It has a creamy, smooth body. The Apricot is apricot right through from start to finish, but is subdued enough to be quite tasty (bronze 1991 GABF). The Cranberry has a pinkish-copper color, a fresh, fruity aroma, well-balanced malt-hop palate, and a very tasty, crisp finish. Woodruff Ale tastes like, well, woodruff, a slightly spicy herb (toned down a little from its early robust woodruff character; silver 1992 GABF).

St. Stan's Brewery & Restaurant
821 L Street, Modesto, 95354

TELEPHONE: RESTAURANT, (209) 524-4PUB; BREWERY, 524-BEER
DIRECTIONS: JUST OFF OF HWY 99; ACROSS FROM THE RED LION HOTEL/CONVENTION CENTER ON HWY 132
HOURS: MON–THUR: 11A.M.–11P.M.; FRI–SAT: TILL MIDNIGHT; SUN: TILL 9P.M.
WHEELCHAIR ACCESS: YES
SMOKING: NO SMOKING INDOORS
ENTERTAINMENT: A VARIETY OF LIVE MUSIC THUR–SAT NIGHTS, TV, DARTS
TOURS: SAT AT 2:30P.M. OR BY APPOINTMENT; SELF-GUIDED TOURS AT ALL TIMES
CREDIT CARDS: AMEX, DISCOVER, MASTERCARD, VISA

From the moment you see friendly little St. Stan standing just inside the entrance quaffing a beer and leaning on the brew menu you know you are in for a good time. Even though he's only two-dimensional, you still can't wait to come inside. Of course, the "real" St. Stan only comes around once a year, learning the ropes of patron sainthood from a friend of his from the north, but his statues and his legendary beer are constant reminders that this place really does have a guardian angel.

The entrance on L Street, looking like a modern cathedral, boasts a two-story brick arch with carved doors below. Set in the soaring glass above the door is a stained-glass replica of one of St. Stan's bottle labels. On the corner is a clock tower with a glockenspiel. St. Stan's covers the entire block in a modern stucco building, with awnings, brick trim, and hops growing right down to the street from the dining balcony.

In addition to the main dining room, there is a hundred-seat banquet room on the second floor and a Biergarten at the street level. The interior is just as elegant, with an oak bar, upholstered chairs and booths, brass lamps, and recessed lighting. Along with the ficus and ferns, you will find hops growing over the bar on an open woodwork platform that supports animated figures, created by Disney artists, of Modesto's favorite fictional friar making beer in a forest with reindeer and the legendary elves who gave him the original formula.

The Abbey appetizers include barbecue drumettes, soft pretzels and nachos, as well as pizzas, salads, and soups, including St. Stan's Alt Beer Soup. There are sandwiches, burgers, and St. Stan's favorite: Aldell's beer sausage and sauerkraut, served on Alt Beer bread. For the larger appetite, they have a grilled sausage platter, barbecued ribs, chicken, and seafood.

Before you leave, stroll through the gift shop, where St. Stan's beer can be sampled and supplies for a complete picnic can be purchased.

THE BREWS

St. Stan's motto, "Conceived in heaven, brewed in California," is an apt description of their beers. In this case, "heaven" means Dusseldorf, Germany, where the German altbier tradition has survived and flourished. It is also the home of Romy Angle, co-owner of St. Stan's.

Founded by Angle and his wife, Garith Helm, St. Stan's opened as the Stanislaus Brewing Co. in 1984. It was located in an almond grove on the outskirts of Modesto. It was the first modern craft brewery in the United States to make German altbiers. In 1990 it reopened in downtown Modesto as a brewpub.

For the first ten years, St. Stan's brewed with a twenty-barrel brewhouse, manufactured locally. In order to keep up with the ever-increasing demand for St. Stan's beers, in 1994 capacity was tripled with the installation of a sixty-barrel brewhouse.

Brewmaster Garith Helm oversees the operation and is assisted by head brewer David Marshall. Both began as homebrewers and have attended classes at the University of California at Davis. American two-row pale and specialty malts are milled at the brewery. Several varieties of American hop and German Hallertauer hop pellets are used. Most of the beers are dry hopped. All of the bottled products are filtered. Usually the beers on tap at the restaurant are served unfiltered, or "virgin," as they call them at the bar. Five to nine beers are on tap at all times, including Red Sky Ale, St. Stan's Amber, and St. Stan's Dark as well as several seasonal beers. They are available in servings of twelve ounces ($2.25), sixteen ounces ($2.65), and sixty-four-ounce pitchers ($8.00). Sampler sets of four beers are available for $2.50. There are twelve-ounce bottled beers to go in the gift shop and beer cubes from the bar.

Red Sky Ale is bright, reddish copper with a fresh, estery, malty aroma and a sweet, caramelized malt palate balanced with a fresh hoppy finish. St. Stan's Amber Alt (1.048) is hazy amber with a citrusy, hop aroma and a very satisfying, complex, malt-hop palate. St. Stan's Dark Alt (1.052) is burnt-orange copper with a complex, estery, fruity aroma and a rich, buttery and complex palate of caramelized and scorched malt with fruity notes. St. Stan's Fest Alt Bier (1.056, served in the winter) is hazy copper with a complex fruity, estery aroma and notes of strawberry, grapefruit, and vanilla, and a big, fresh hoppy taste backed by a strong malt flavor and followed by a zesty, bitter, hoppy finish. St. Stan's Graffiti Wheat (1.040, with a fifty-fifty mixture of malted wheat and barley) tends to be hoppy, fruity, and complex—the recipe changes slightly each year. It is brewed in the late spring and summer for the annual Modesto Graffiti Festival, held the first week in June. Each year's bottle label features a 1950s classic car.

Other beers include Whistle Stop Ale (pale ale), St. Stan's Light (1.030, lager), St. Stan's Barley Wine (1.075), Pumpkin Ale, Porter, and Raspberry Wheat.

EL TORO BREWING CO.
17370 Hill Road, Morgan Hill, 95037

TELEPHONE: (408) 778-BREW
DIRECTIONS: FROM U.S. 101, TAKE THE EAST DUNNE AVENUE EXIT; TURN LEFT ON HILL ROAD; IT'S ON THE RIGHT
TOURS: WALK-INS ACCEPTED MON–FRI, 11A.M.–5P.M.

In the wine country a few miles south of San Jose lies the village of Morgan Hill. Geno and Cindy Acevedo live on a quiet street just at the base of the highest peak in the area, El Toro. Geno worked as an aeronautical engineer at McDonnell-Douglas and he and Cindy made beer at home as a hobby for many years.

Over the years they had won numerous ribbons at homebrewing competitions. Finally, they decided they had the expertise to start their own brewery and join the growing craft-brewing industry. They must have been right—within six months after opening they won a gold medal in the English pale ale category for their El Toro Oro at the Great American Beer Festival.

The Acevedos built their brewery on the property next to their house. They purchased a seventeen-barrel system from Newlands Manufacturing and began distributing their beers in April 1994. Cindy does the paperwork, and the couple shares the brewing responsibilities. In 1995 they installed a bottling line and began distributing in twelve-ounce bottles as well as kegs.

THE BREWS
The Acevedos are making two beers on a regular basis: El Toro Oro and Poppy Jasper Amber Beer. The latter is named for a rock that is only found in the Morgan Hill area. They have experimented with many seasonal beers, making Peach Ale, Black Raspberry Ale, Raspberry Ale, Kick Ace Barleywine, Kellerbier Lager, and India Pale Ale. All of the beers are filtered, except for the Barleywine and the Kellerbier Lager. The latter is cask-conditioned.

CARMEL BREWING CO.
1044 Harkins Road, Salinas, 93091

TELEPHONE: (408) 771-ALES;
FAX, 771-0651
DIRECTIONS: FROM U.S. 101 IN SALINAS, TAKE THE MONTEREY PENINSULA EXIT (SANBORN ROAD); RIGHT ON SANBORN; LEFT ON ABBOTT STREET; THEN RIGHT ON HARKINS ROAD
TOURS: TUE–THUR: 2–4P.M.; TASTING ROOM OPEN FROM NOON– 5P.M., MON–FRI

Small California wineries set the trend in the sixties. With the craft brewing boom in the nineties, it is fitting that the first craft brewery in the Salinas valley is located in the offices and storage area of the old Lockwood Vineyard. Salinas is in the heart of Steinbeck country, and I think the author, being a man of the people, would have approved of the latest turn of events. After all, beer is the drink of the people.

The Carmel Brewing Company was founded in 1994 by Paul Tarantino, a native of the Carmel valley. Paul discovered good beer as a student at Oregon State University. While living in Corvallis, he made his first batch of beer in his apartment and discovered the magic of brewing. After graduation, he returned to California with plans to open his own brewery. Paul consulted with Karl Strauss, former vice president of production at Pabst Brewing. While in Oregon, Paul also met Angela Mussio, who became an enthusiastic advocate and helped Paul open the brewery; she is now in charge of sales and marketing. With financial backing from his father, Paul was able to open his own brewery at the age of only twenty-three. The first kegs rolled out the door in March of 1995.

THE BREWS

The beers are made by brewmaster Bob Weisskirchen, formerly brewmaster at Blitz Weinhard's Brewing in Portland, Oregon. Bob is brewing with a thirty-barrel brewhouse manufactured by Specific Mechanical Systems. He does consecutive batches, which are racked to sixty-barrel fermenters. All American malts and pellet hops are used. The two all-season beers are Mission Hefeweizen Wheat Ale (1.052, an unfiltered, American wheat beer) and Cypress Amber Ale (1.048, a filtered light ale). Seasonal ales are planned. The beers are currently distributed in kegs and twelve-ounce bottles.

Santa Cruz Brewing Co. & Front Street Pub

516 Front Street, Santa Cruz, 95060

TELEPHONE: (408) 429-8838; FAX, 429-8915

DIRECTIONS: Coming into town on Ocean Street, turn right on Water, cross the San Lorenzo River, and then turn left on Front Street. It's on the left

HOURS: Sun–Thur: 11:30A.M.–midnight; Fri–Sat: till 12:30A.M.

WHEELCHAIR ACCESS: Yes

SMOKING: None

ENTERTAINMENT: Live music (blues, country), TV, darts

TOURS: Drop-ins accepted; by appointment for large groups

CREDIT CARDS: Discover, MasterCard, Visa

Since 1986, the father and son team of Gerry and Bernard Turgeon have provided Santa Cruz with a downtown brewpub with a quaint, English atmosphere, a warm, welcoming feel, and decor rooted in Santa Cruz's maritime past.

The front of the pub displays its name and logo in Victorian lettering on windows shaded by canvas awnings. The interior is open and welcoming, with exposed trusses, blonde oak, ferns, and potted—or should we say basketed—evergreens. Above the bar is a shake roof topped by a working brass lighthouse beacon. The nautical theme is further carried by prints of lighthouses, brass fittings, and oak paneling. The polished oak bar is accented by a row of glass bricks lighted from behind and a brass foot rail the length of the bar. A surprising piece of detail behind the bar is the facade from a deserted Coast Guard lighthouse near the brewery.

Front Street Pub is also a survivor of the 1989 Loma Prieta earthquake, and after repairs was once again a beacon for its longtime patrons, who consider this place almost like another home.

The menu, decorated in nautical art, starts off with munchies such as beer bread and fog-bound chili, specialties such as shark bites (shark nuggets dipped in beer batter and deep fried), ploughman's lunch, and salads. Or, try their Speidies™—spicy, marinated pork on a stick, charbroiled and served on Italian bread. Their sandwich menu is enticing—try the beer link, a plump Polish sausage steamed in their own Pacific Porter, a calamari sandwich, or a "Surf Burger," fresh red snapper charbroiled and served on a French roll with homemade tartar sauce.

Another of the unique offerings of the Front Street Pub is the "Prohibition Style" homebrewed root beer, served up cold and frosty. Before you go, don't forget to ask what the daily desserts are—rumor has it they are beyond comparison.

THE BREWS

The beers at Front Street are made by Scotty Morgan, an award-winning homebrewer who is also a partner and cofounder of the brewpub, with the assistance of head brewer Alex Kohrt. They make the beers on a seven-barrel system made by JV Northwest and the Pub. American two-row pale and specialty malts are milled at the brewery. Scottie prefers to use American leaf hops to the pellets. The wort is normally strained through a hop back in order to impart more hop flavor and aroma. All of the beers are filtered except for the wheat, porter, and stout. In 1994, eighteen hundred barrels were produced.

Most of the beers at Front Street are lagers, which Scotty cold conditions for at least two weeks longer than he does the ales. I found them smooth, yet with an interesting depth to their character, due in part, perhaps, to the multiple-step infusion mash he employs. The primary fermentation takes place in open tanks.

Six-ounce samples are available for $1.25. Other serving sizes are ten ounces ($2.25), a true pint ($3.25), a twenty-two-ounce glass ($3.75), and pitchers ($7.75). Beer is available to go in twenty-two-ounce bottles.

Front Street features three regular beers—a lager, amber, and porter—plus several rotationals, for a total of five to seven beers on tap. Lighthouse Lager (1.046) is bright gold with a sweet malty entry and a crisp, hoppy finish. Lighthouse Amber (1.048) is copper with plentiful roasted malts in the palate and a hoppy finish. Pacific Porter (1.055) is dark brown to black with a reddish tint and a light brown creamy head. The palate is of sweet, deeply roasted malts with notes of chocolate and coffee and a bittersweet finish. Palookaville Lager has a very compact head with a fluffy top and a smooth, dry palate. Scott's Big Wheat (1.060) is cloudy gold, and has a yeasty aroma with a delicious and refreshing, delicately complex malt palate and some hop bitterness in the finish. Lighthouse Dark Lager (1.052) has a nutty brown color and a deliciously drinkable, malty palate. Beacon Bock (1.060) is a dark reddish-brown with a complex, roasted malt palate. Pacific Stout (1.073) is black with a rich, creamy, malty palate. Beacon Barley Wine (1.095) is deep gold with a fruity-malty aroma. It is very sweet and malty with a full body and ample bitterness in the finish.

Seabright Brewery Pub & Restaurant

519 Seabright Avenue #107, Santa Cruz, 95062

TELEPHONE: (408) 426-2739
DIRECTIONS: Corner of Murray Street; two blocks from beach, between Harbor & Beach Boardwalk
HOURS: Sun–Thur: 11:30a.m.–midnight; Fri–Sat: till 12:30a.m.
WHEELCHAIR ACCESS: Yes
SMOKING: No smoking indoors
ENTERTAINMENT: Live music (blues, jazz), TV
TOURS: Drop in, appointments preferred
CREDIT CARDS: MasterCard, Visa

If variety in beer styles is what you are looking for, Santa Cruz is the place to visit. Each of the three brewpubs—Front Street, Live Soup, and Seabright—has its own specialty. Front Street highlights its fine lagers, although it offers ales as well; Live Soup has a Belgian accent to its ales; and Seabright offers a vast array of well-made American-style ales.

The Seabright Brewery resembles a modern, attractive shopping center or office building, which is done in "desert deco" with white stucco walls, big sun-worshiping windows, and bicycles parked in front. The bright, airy design is carried inside as well. Recessed as though part of the architecture of the building, the big oak bar offers respite from the traffic and the crowds. The "Sunny California" look is echoed throughout with gaily colored tiles setting off the work of local artists. The outdoor patio, overlooking East Cliff Drive, is furnished with umbrella tables and patio chairs, adding to the coastal ambience. Seabright's crowd is made up of local surfers, students, and sailors from the nearby yacht club, as well as tourists. Live music is available on weekends with Sunday jazz on the patio.

They offer pub sandwiches, salads, shrimp baskets, pastas, and the ploughman's lunch. Appetizers include Buffalo wings, calamari, and frijole melt, as well as soups, salads, and pizzas. An interesting note: This is probably the only place in town offering a full-pound burger. But the best of all is the chili. Douglas Gruen, chef extraordinaire, boasts first prize at the 1989 Santa Cruz Chili Cook-off for his chili simmered in stout.

Whether walking the few minutes from the beach or looking for a quiet oasis from the hustle and bustle of Santa Cruz, Seabright Brewery Pub and Restaurant is the "coolest" place in town. For real.

THE BREWS

Since opening in May 1988, Seabright Brewery has provided a great variety of beer styles, most of them rotating, which invites beer fans to stop to check out the latest specials. Brewer Will Turner brews on a seven-barrel system manufactured by JV Northwest. He uses exclusively American two-row pale and specialty malts, which are milled at the brewery. Several varieties of American pellet hops are used, as well as leaf hops for flavoring in some of the hoppier beers. Most of the beers are filtered; however, at least one of the beers is dry hopped and served unfiltered from a beer engine. About twelve hundred barrels were produced in 1994.

Normally, seven to ten beers are on tap at any given time. The three regulars are Pelican Pale Ale (1.052), Seabright Amber (1.052), and Oatmeal Stout (1.064). The Pelican Pale is bright gold with a well-balanced palate of complex malts and fresh hops in the finish. The Amber is medium copper with a little more roastiness than the pale. Seabright Oatmeal Stout is brown to black with a short, creamy brown head, and a delicious, complex, bittersweet finish, with notes of rich chocolate. Holy Grail Ale is an amber ale with a light roasted maltiness and light hops. The ESB is unfiltered and dry hopped and has an attractive, bright copper color, a full body, and a hearty balance of roasted malts and hops with notes of butterscotch. Blackcat Stout is even sweeter, with a thick body and notes of licorice. The Barleywine is cloudy orange with a fresh, fruity aroma and a very hoppy palate, but not too bitter. It is unfiltered and dry hopped. Other rotational beers that are served frequently include Anniversary Ale, Banty Rooster, Pleasure Point Porter, and Seabright Weizenbock.

The beers are available in six-ounce samplers ($1.00 each), twelve-ounce servings ($2.25), pints ($3.00), and pitchers ($7.25). Prices for specialty beers are slightly higher. Prices are lowered for happy hour, Wednesday to Friday from 4:00 to 6:00 P.M. Tuesday is "neighborhood night," with discounts all night. Beer is available for take out in thirty-two-ounce jars.

Seabright has won numerous medals at the GABF, including silver for the Amber in 1991, silver for the Porter and the Banty Rooster in 1992; gold in 1991 and a silver in 1992 for the IPA, gold for the Oatmeal Stout in 1992 and 1993, and bronze for DeLaveaga Red Ale in 1994.

El Dorado Brewing Co.
157 West Adams Street, Stockton, 95204

TELEPHONE: (209) 948-ALES;
FAX, 948-4924
DIRECTIONS: From I-5, take the Pershing Avenue exit; go north on Pershing; then turn right on Harding Way, left on Pacific Avenue, and right on West Adams
HOURS: Sun–Thur: 11 a.m.–11 p.m.; Fri–Sat: till midnight
WHEELCHAIR ACCESS: Yes
SMOKING: No smoking indoors
ENTERTAINMENT: Live music (blues, jazz, rock) Fri–Sun evenings
TOURS: On a drop-in basis or by appointment
CREDIT CARDS: Discover, MasterCard, Visa

Stockton has a long tradition of brewing that goes back to 1853, when Peter and Daniel Rothenbush, early German immigrants, founded the El Dorado Brewing Co. Stockton, being the closest inland port to the gold fields, was the perfect spot to make beer for the thirsty miners. Later, during Prohibition, El Dorado managed to stay open making fruit juices and near beer. When Prohibition was repealed, the brewery returned to making traditional beers, such as German pilsners and bocks and light and dark English ales. Competition from the national breweries proved to be even harder than Prohibition, and the brewery finally closed in 1955.

Since the early days of the brewing renaissance, Stocktonians had to drive a long way for a good beer—either thirty-five miles to St. Stan's in Modesto or forty-five miles to Hogshead or Rubicon in Sacramento. All that changed in July 1994 when Creighton Younnel opened the new El Dorado Brewing Co., almost forty years since the closing of the original brewery.

Because the original brewery building was torn down in 1958, Creighton had to find another structure, and he moved into a 1930s warehouse that had at one time served as a porno theater. Preferring to remind customers of the city's brewing heritage, Creighton adorned the brick walls with beautiful, oversize recreations of the original Valley Girl posters from the first El Dorado Brewery. The new brewpub has a comfortable, welcoming feel. It is contained in one great room with high raft-and-timber ceilings and bare-brick walls. The square bar sits near the middle and features an antique Indian motorcycle. For warm weather, there is a covered patio with seating for fifty. The clientele is a mixture of students, working people, and professionals, young and old alike.

They offer several appetizers as well as soups and salads. Beyond that, there are several sandwiches, burgers, pizzas (made with sourdough crust), and pastas. Entrees include blackened chicken breast, Baja stir fry, and rib-eye steak.

THE BREWS

Head brewer Blake Bomben makes his beers on a seven-barrel brewhouse manufactured by Cross Distributing, with closed fermenters that are seven and fourteen barrels in size. Blake says he first discovered homebrewing while majoring in chemical engineering at the University of California at Davis. He later obtained a degree in fermentation science and worked for the R. H. Phillips Winery.

Blake uses a base of two-row domestic pale malts that are milled at the brewery, to which he adds domestic and imported specialty malts. He uses both domestic and imported pellet hops. A hop back is used to impart hop flavor and aroma to the beers. All of the beers are filtered except for the mild ale and some of the wheat beers.

Normally, four regular beers are on tap, plus a seasonal. Beers are available in twelve-ounce ($2.25) and sixteen-ounce ($2.75) glasses and pitchers ($9.00). Samplers cost 75¢. Beer is available for take out in gallon boxes.

The Miracle Mile Mild is hazy gold with a fruity aroma and a sweet, malty, and fruity palate. Valley Brew Pale Wheat is clear gold with a sweet malty entry; it finishes smooth and lightly hoppy. Cherry Wheat is cloudy amber with medium roasted malts, light hops, and fruity notes. Stockton Ports Pale Ale is bright copper with plenty of roasted malt balanced by a fresh hoppy bitterness. Indian Red has a bright, deep reddish-copper color and a fresh Cascade palate with roasted malts in the background. Black Cat Stout is dark brown to black with an initial bittersweet, deeply roasted malt palate and a drying, burnt-barley finish (served under a nitrogen-CO_2 mix). Other seasonals include Apricot Wheat, Strong Amber Ale, and ESB.

North Coast and Wine Country

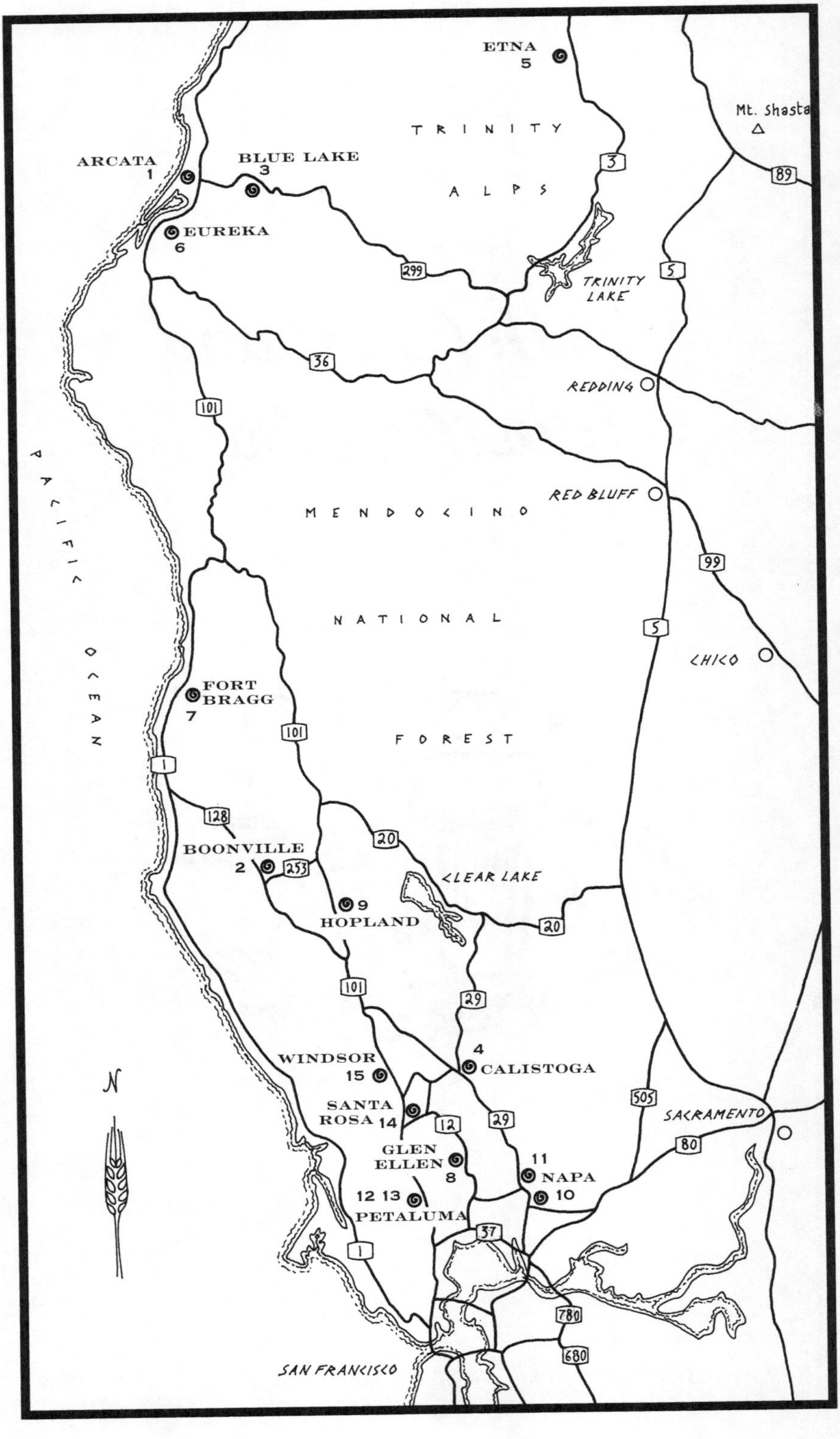
ETNA
5
TRINITY
ALPS
Mt. Shasta
ARCATA
1
BLUE LAKE
3
EUREKA
6
TRINITY LAKE
REDDING
PACIFIC OCEAN
RED BLUFF
MENDOCINO
NATIONAL
FOREST
CHICO
FORT BRAGG
7
BOONVILLE
2
CLEAR LAKE
9
HOPLAND
WINDSOR
15
4
CALISTOGA
SANTA ROSA
14
SACRAMENTO
GLEN ELLEN
8
11
NAPA
10
12 13
PETALUMA
SAN FRANCISCO
N
3
89
299
5
36
101
99
1
128
20
253
29
505
12
80
37
780
680

NORTH COAST AND WINE COUNTRY

CITY	BREWERY (MAP KEY)	PAGE
ARCATA	HUMBOLDT BREWERY CO. (1)	108
BLUE LAKE	MAD RIVER BREWING CO. (2)	109
BOONVILLE	ANDERSON VALLEY BREWERY & BUCKHORN SALOON (3)	111
CALISTOGA	CALISTOGA INN & NAPA VALLEY BREWING CO. (4)	114
ETNA	ETNA BREWERY (5)	116
EUREKA	LOST COAST BREWERY & CAFÉ (6)	117
FORT BRAGG	NORTH COAST BREWING CO. (7)	119
GLEN ELLEN	HUMES BREWING CO. (8)	122
HOPLAND	MENDOCINO BREWING CO. & HOPLAND BREWERY, BREWPUB & BEER GARDEN (9)	123
NAPA	DOWNTOWN JOE'S BREWERY & RESTAURANT (10)	125
	NAPA VALLEY ALE WORKS (11)	127
PETALUMA	DEMPSEY'S ALE HOUSE & SONOMA BREWING CO. (12)	128
	LAGUNITAS BREWING CO. (13)	130
SANTA ROSA	SANTA ROSA BREWING CO. (14)	131
WINDSOR	MOONLIGHT BREWING CO. (15)	133

Humboldt Brewery Co.
856 Tenth Street, Arcata, 95521

TELEPHONE: (707) 826-BREW; FAX, 826-2045
DIRECTIONS: Going north on Hwy 101, take the 14th Street exit and go left, turn left on H Street and then right on 10th Street. It's one block from the historic Plaza in downtown Arcata.
HOURS: Mon–Thur: noon–11 p.m.; Fri–Sat: till 2 a.m.; Sun: till 10 p.m.
WHEELCHAIR ACCESS: Yes
SMOKING: None
ENTERTAINMENT: Live music (blues, reggae, psychedelic pop) Fri & Sat, TV
TOURS: Appointments are preferred
CREDIT CARDS: MasterCard, Visa

Humboldt Brewing Company is just a couple of blocks off Highway 101 in downtown Arcata, near shopping and the town plaza. The exterior is modern and businesslike. Step inside, though, and the wood-and-brick interior welcomes you to another world. There is an extensive, well-scattered collection of glass beer mugs and glasses—some of them elegant enough to pass for crystal. The owners are Mario and Vince Celotta, and since Mario was a linebacker for the Oakland Raiders, you can expect plenty of sports memorabilia as well. Above the doorway are old footballs, with antique beer posters, sports pictures and pictures of athletes and celebrities adorning the walls. Of course, a big-screen TV for viewing sports is a must. The wooden bar sports English beer pumps called beer engines, and there is a view of the brewery behind glass.

The large dining area is separate from the bar and contains a cozy stone fireplace that is warm and welcoming. The menu offers pub fare but on a much grander scale. To start with, try the Red Nectar bayou shrimp in quarter-pound increments, which is cooked in Red Nectar Ale and sauteed in bayou chili spice, or the beer-battered zucchini. The salads are more than lettuce and dressing: try the smoked turkey salad, the smoked albacore salad, or the spinach bacon salad.

If your appetite needs more attention, the burgers and sandwiches leave no room for complaint and feature Humboldt's famous cajun house spices. Try a cheeseburger smothered in their chainsaw chili or a grilled cajun chicken sandwich. For the vegetarian, they serve the Earth Nut Pickpocket Pita, a curried garbanzo bean pattie mixed with sunflower seeds and walnuts and then grilled. For dessert, the cream cheese apple cake comes highly recommended!

THE BREWS
Before coming to Humboldt, brewmaster Steve Parkes received his de-

gree in brewing at Heriot Watt University in Edinburgh, Scotland. He has brewed at Oxford Brewing in Maryland, and at three breweries in Britain.

The beers are made with a fifty-barrel brewhouse and several hundred-barrel fermenters. American malts, milled at the brewery, are used, with the exception of English crystal malt, used because it gives a redder color than its American counterpart. A variety of domestic pellet hops are used, with Cascade and Mount Hood predominating. All of the beers are filtered, with the exception of the stout. In 1994, 14,700 barrels were produced; about five hundred barrels were sold in the pub.

Normally four beers are on tap at a time. Beers are available in eight-ounce servings ($1.75), pints ($2.75), and pitchers ($6.95). Samplers are available at 50¢ each.

Gold Rush Pale Ale (1.048) is bright gold with a fresh, hoppy palate (served very cold). Red Nectar (1.055, silver 1993 GABF) is clear, orangish-copper with a delicate, fruity-flowery aroma and a nicely balanced and complex palate of roasted malt and fresh hops with notes of fresh strawberries. The Oatmeal Stout (1.060, gold 1988 GABF) is black with a creamy brown head and a smooth, roasty-toffee palate and a soft mouthfeel. Black Cherry Stout is black with a creamy brown head and a roasted malt and black cherry palate. Cheshire Cat Barley Wine (1.095) is a very deep reddish copper with a sweet, malty, fruity entry and a sweet, malty, and spicy finish with an alcoholic warmth. They also make Gold Nectar.

MAD RIVER BREWING CO.

195 Taylor Way (P.O. Box 948), Blue Lake, 95525

TELEPHONE: (707) 668-4151; FAX, 668-4297

DIRECTIONS: FROM HWY 101, TAKE HWY 299; GO 7 MILES TO THE BLUE LAKE EXIT; TAKE THE SECOND RIGHT (GREENWOOD); FOLLOW SIGNS TO THE INDUSTRIAL PARK; CROSS RAILROAD TRACKS; FROM HATCHERY WAY, TURN RIGHT ON TAYLOR WAY. IT IS NEAR THE MAD RIVER FISH HATCHERY

TOURS: SAT AT 2 & 4 P.M. OR BY APPOINTMENT

Bob Smith, founder, general manager and brewmaster of Mad River Brewing has paid his dues to the American beer renaissance. Judging from the quality of his beer, those long, hard years of toil and learning have paid off. If you haven't had his extra stout, you haven't lived. I once purchased a bottle at a liquor store in Eureka. As I was driving east on Route 299 I saw a nice place to pull over beside the Trinity River. The beauty of the river and the beer will be one of those moments I will always remember.

Bob made beer at home for more than twenty years and has won numerous homebrewing awards. He was involved in the founding of the first microbrewery in the country, New Albion Brewing, later was involved in the founding of Sierra Nevada Brewing, and has also worked at Mendocino, Humboldt, and Lost Coast breweries. In December 1990 he opened his own brewery on the banks of the Mad River, with the old mash tun and brew kettle from the Sierra Nevada Brewing Co.

THE BREWS

The beers are double batched from the seventeen-barrel brew kettle into thirty-five-barrel, open flat-bed fermenters. From there, the beer is triple batched into hundred-barrel conditioning tanks. From the conditioning tanks the beer is racked to the bright beer tank where it is carbonated and partially filtered with a German paper pad filter. The brewing is done by head brewer Bryan Bohannan and two assistants. In 1994 the brewery produced nearly seven thousand barrels.

All American, two-row pale and specialty malts are used, as well as five different domestic hops—Cluster, Chinook, Cascade, Tettnanger, and Willamette. One beer, the Jamaica Red, is dry hopped in the fermenter.

The beers are packaged in twelve-ounce bottles and kegs. They are distributed throughout California as well as in Oregon, Washington, Alaska, Hawaii, Arizona, Nevada, Colorado, Maryland, and Virginia. You can also buy beer directly from the brewery, which also sells ingredients for homebrewing (pale and specialty malts, leaf hops, and free yeast).

Mad River currently makes four brands. Steel Head Extra Pale Ale is bright gold with very active carbonation. It has a fresh fruity-yeasty aroma and a sweet malt palate, balanced by a long, hoppy, bitter finish. Jamaica Brand Red Ale is dark auburn with a light, roasted-malt aroma, a deeply roasted malt palate, and very satisfying, dry, hoppy, and slightly burnt finish. Steel Head Extra Stout has marvelous eye appeal, with a deep brown to black color and a dark brown, creamy head. The aroma is mouthwatering, roasted malt mixed with sweet chocolate. The palate is very rich and very big, with deeply roasted to burnt malt, espresso coffee, and a hint of chocolate. John Barleycorn Barleywine, which I did not sample, received its name from a pagan legend in which John Barleycorn was killed with the reaping of the barley, and his spirit is re-created with the making of beer.

Anderson Valley Brewery & Buckhorn Saloon

14081 Highway 128 (P. O. Box 505), Boonville, 95415

TELEPHONE: (707) 895-BEER; FAX, 895-2353
DIRECTIONS: It's in the center of town, on the right side of Hwy 128 as you drive north
HOURS: Sun, Mon, Thur: 11a.m.–9p.m.; Fri & Sat: till 11p.m.; closed Tue and Wed during the off season (Dec-March)
WHEELCHAIR ACCESS: Yes
SMOKING: None
ENTERTAINMENT: Darts, horseshoes, table tennis, TV
TOURS: Usually afternoons & weekends; call for an appointment
CREDIT CARDS: Visa, MasterCard

They say getting there is half the fun. But in the case of Mendocino, that mecca of foggy cliffs and Victorian gift shops, getting there is almost all the fun. That's because the village of Boonville is on the way to Mendocino. Exiting Highway 101 at Cloverdale, Highway 128 runs a pleasant twenty-five miles north through apple orchards, vineyards, cattle and sheep ranches, and redwoods to Boonville, home of Anderson Valley Brewery & Buckhorn Saloon.

And half the fun just got twice as good. The Anderson Valley Brewery is in the process of building a second brewery about a zillion times bigger than the first. The owners plan to experiment with growing their own hops and raspberries to use as ingredients for their beer.

The Anderson Valley Brewery was started in 1987 by local chiropractor Ken Allen and his wife, Kim, on the site of the Buckhorn Saloon (built in 1873), the oldest bar in town. The gift shop in front occupies the site of the original saloon; the rest of the building is new and was the first building in California designed as a brewpub. From the outside, it has a rustic, stained-cedar look; a gray grain silo sits in front with a giant Anderson Valley bottle label painted on the side. Inside are skylights and windows that look on the beer garden and the picturesque mountains beyond. During the summer the beer garden offers horseshoe pitching. For the birdwatcher, there are several hummingbird feeders just outside the windows—the owners are just as nice to our feathered friends as they are to beer lovers.

The walls are hung with signs from breweries of old plus more than a hundred beer T-shirts from newer breweries. Be careful when sitting down at the bar—the stools are topped with used tractor seats with a saddle horn that sticks up in the front. The bar was handmade from locally grown oak and walnut. A second floor offers additional seating during busy times.

The brewpub's cuisine features a variety of items prepared with the house beers. Deep Enders Chicken is made with the porter, fisherman's platter is made with their wheat beer, and chili con Barney is made with their stout. The lunch menu offers a variety of appetizers, sandwiches, burgers, salads, and a few entrees. A more substantial menu is available for dinner. If you brought the kids along, they also make their own root beer.

Although not originally from Boonville, Ken and Kim have gone native, so to speak. Not only have they named their beers after the local dialect, called Boontling, they have even placed a sign behind the bar that reads, "It's not just shy sluggin' gorms neemer!" Which in Boontling means, "It's not just for breakfast anymore."

During the 1880s, townfolk who wanted to keep out-of-towners out of their affairs invented their own language. During years of isolation and boredom, the locals gradually enlarged the vocabulary to the point where they even have a dictionary for it. So, be careful if you have to ask someone for directions. You might not understand the reply.

THE BREWS

Brewmaster Ken Allen recently turned over the brewing duties to his son, Loren. Along with several assistants, Loren brews downstairs from the saloon on a ten-barrel system, which has been pieced together over the years from various sources, including dairy farms. In order to keep up with demand they are brewing two batches five or six days a week, and they sometimes even manage to squeeze in a third batch before going to bed. In 1994, forty-five hundred barrels were produced—quite an accomplishment for such a small system. The beers are distributed in more than twenty states.

A variety of domestic malts and pelletized hops are used to make the beers. The water source is an eighty-foot-deep well, rich in bicarbonates, located directly beneath the building. With the exception of the Barney Flats Oatmeal Stout, all the beers are filtered.

Beers are available in five-ounce ($1.30), ten-ounce ($1.90), and sixteen-ounce servings ($2.65), as well as pitchers ($7.65). Specials (Belk's, Barney Flats, Oktoberfest, and Raspberry Wheat) cost a little more. Usually eight beers are on tap at a time. Several sizes of kegs and twenty-two-ounce bottles are available for take out.

The beers at Anderson Valley Brewing are simply yummy. So yummy, in fact, that the story is told of a cyclist who parked his bicycle outside the saloon, drank a pitcher of each offering (that's eight pitchers!), and then had a second pitcher of his favorite, Barney Flats. When he was finished, the cyclist rose from the bar with a grin, wobbled out to his bicycle (after a detour to the men's room), and rode off down the highway whistling "Waltzing Mathilda." He hasn't been seen or heard from since.

The lightest selection is High Rollers Wheat Beer (1.051), named after a region of the Anderson Valley. It is a hazy, faintly greenish-gold brew, with a tart and fruity palate, made with a fifty-fifty mix of wheat and malted barley. Poleeko Gold (1.052), a well-balanced, American pale ale, starts out sweet and malty and finishes hoppy-citrusy and crisp. It is named for the Poleekers, residents of the village of Philo, the capital of the Blue Jay region. Boont Amber (1.055) is bright copper, with a full body, a goodly dose of caramel malt flavor, and a hint of nuttiness. It is named for the town of Boonville. Belk's Extra Special Bitter (1.062, gold 1994 GABF) is a light amber with a mouth-watering, fresh hoppy quality combined with roasted malts and a fresh citrusy finish—it's named for the Belk region, a scenic valley northeast of Boonville. The Raspberry Wheat is cloudy red with a clean, fresh raspberry flavor. It is made with whole, fresh raspberries. Deep Enders Porter (1.052) is dark and rich with a bittersweet, espresso-chocolate finish. Deep Enders is named for the residents of the Iteville region of the valley. Winter Solstice is brewed for the Christmas holiday. Reddish copper in color, it has a full body with a spicy, cinnamon palate. The suds de résistance is the Barney Flats Oatmeal Stout (1.063), a rich stout with a silky body, brown to black in color and well endowed with fresh hops and deeply roasted malt. An Oktoberfest is also made in the autumn, and a Barley Wine Horn of the Beer (1.099) at other times.

CALISTOGA INN & NAPA VALLEY BREWING CO.
1250 Lincoln Avenue, Calistoga, 94515

TELEPHONE: (707) 942-4101; FAX, 942-4914
DIRECTIONS: ON THE CORNER OF LINCOLN AND CEDAR IN DOWNTOWN CALISTOGA
HOURS: DAILY: 11:30A.M.–CLOSING
WHEELCHAIR ACCESS: YES
SMOKING: NO SMOKING INDOORS
ENTERTAINMENT: OCCASIONAL LIVE MUSIC (ROCK, REGGAE, JAZZ), TV, DARTS
TOURS: BY APPOINTMENT
CREDIT CARDS: AMEX, MASTERCARD, VISA

Calistoga is one of those delightful little towns not to be missed on your trip through California's wine country. The town was founded in 1859 when Samuel Brannan built an opulent spa here. Mud baths and hot-water pools still flourish. Other attractions include a nearby geyser and petrified forest, hang gliding for the more adventurous, or just window shopping in the old downtown. If you choose to stay overnight, there are several charming hotels and restaurants.

The Calistoga Inn is a delightful restaurant brewery/bed and breakfast, located near the west end of Lincoln Avenue. It is housed in a white Swiss chalet-style building that dates to the turn of the century. While others are soaking in hot mud and sipping champagne, this is the place for the beer lover to relax and nurse a brew in one of California's most graceful and tranquil beer gardens.

When the brewery was added to the inn by former owner Phil Rogers, he put the brewing equipment in the original water tower beside the Napa River and built a patio between the tower, the inn and the river. The old water tower, the patio with potted flowers and trailing vines, and the soft tinkling sound of water from the fountain are conducive to relaxation and contemplation.

Soon after adding the brewery, Rogers was asked why he built a brewpub instead of a winery—he replied, "It takes a lot of beer to make good wine, there was too much competition in wine in the valley, and it was very hot, so the demand for a good, fresh, locally made beer was great." The new owners are the Nilsson and Dunsford families, who have left the brewpub just as Rogers created it.

The three dining rooms are as warm as the staff is friendly, having a European feel with white tablecloths, antique porcelain dishes displayed on the walls, and windows with flower boxes either looking onto Lincoln Avenue or the beer garden. The bar is in a separate room featuring old wooden floors and a handsome mahogany bar and railing.

The restaurant offers a great variety of regional, seafood, and seasonal dishes with several daily specials. Start with an ample selection of appetizers and finger food, including Malpeque oysters on the half shell, grilled herb polenta, quesadilla, grilled crab cake, Buffalo Wings, or calamari. Entrees include such choice items as lemon garlic chicken, Jamaican jerk chicken, fillet mignon, tri-tip sirloin, and a Tillamook cheeseburger, all grilled over hardwood. In addition, there is an assortment of salads, soups, and desserts. Dinner reservations are advised.

If you are interested in spending the night, rooms range from $49 to $60 and include a complimentary pint of fresh beer.

THE BREWS

Head brewer Randy Gremp, a resident of Calistoga for fourteen years, started out homebrewing before coming to the Napa Valley Brewing Co. He brews on a seven-barrel system. Because of the long distance between the brewery and the pub, the beers are served from kegs. He uses a combination of domestic and imported malts. The three regular beers (Golden Lager, Red Ale, and wheat) use domestic pale malt and imported crystal malts. The specialty beers are made with imported English and Belgian malts. Randy uses about ten different pellet hops, all of them domestic, with the exception of East Kent Goldings from England, which he uses in some the specialty beers. He dry hops the Golden Lager, ESB, and the IPA. The Golden Lager and the Red Ale are filtered; the rest are unfiltered.

During the tourist season (May to September) three beers are on tap. In the off-season, when demand diminishes, as many as six beers may be on tap. Beers are available in six-ounce sampler ($1.25) and pint glasses ($3.25). During happy hour (Mon to Fri, 4:00-6:00 P.M.) pints are $2.00. Beer is available for take out in twenty-two-ounce bottles and one-gallon beer cubes.

Randy makes a delightful, fresh Wheat Ale (1.050), which is hazy gold with a hoppy floral aroma and a tart and fruity palate—a wonderful treat on a warm summer day. It's made with a fifty-fifty blend of wheat and barley malt (gold 1994 GABF). Calistoga Golden Lager (1.050) is bright gold with a fresh floral aroma and a fresh, fruity-hoppy palate (Randy dry hops it with domestic Tettnanger). Calistoga Red Ale (1.056) has a beautiful, reddish-copper color, a toasty, malty palate and a fresh, hoppy finish (bronze 1991 GABF). The latter is outdone by a well-balanced Extra Special Bitter with an exhilarating, fruity nose and a clean, malty palate, with a hefty dollop of hops in the finish. Next is a delightful porter with a faint coffee aroma and loads of coffee and chocolate in the mouth and a wonderful, rich, bittersweet finish. But the best of all is the fruity and potent Old Faithful Barleywine (1.104)—aged for a full year to let the flavors mellow.

ETNA BREWERY
131 Callahan Street, Etna, 96027

TELEPHONE: (916) 467-5277
DIRECTIONS: IN DOWNTOWN ETNA (PLEASE CALL FOR MORE SPECIFIC DIRECTIONS)
TOURS: OPEN HOUSE SAT FROM 1–5 P.M., OR BY APPOINTMENT

Etna is one of northern California's hidden gems—better visit it before it's discovered. Tucked away in the Scott Valley, surrounded by high mountains, the village of Etna is much like it was in the early twentieth century when it was the home of the original Etna Brewery. Founded by Charles F. Kappler in 1872, the brewery was highly successful, garnering national and international awards for its beers. It closed, never to reopen, when Prohibition became the law of the land in 1919.

Seventy-one years later, local rancher Andrew Hurlimann and his wife, Brenda, reestablished the brewing tradition in Etna. Andrew first began homebrewing while a student at Chico State University. As he continued to brew, he won awards at local and national homebrew competitions. In 1987 Andrew and Brenda purchased the property where the original Etna Brewery had been located and set about to start their own brewery. Andrew attended a two-day, intensive course on brewing at the University of California at Davis and traveled around California visiting breweries to learn the business. After three years of hard work, the brewery went into production in May of 1990. Like its predecessor, the new Etna Brewery has already captured a coveted award. In 1994 at a beer festival held in Sacramento and sponsored by the Sutter Symphony, in a lopsided vote, Etna won the Sacramento Peoples Choice Award for having the best beer at the festival.

Photographs of the old brewery hang on the walls of the tasting room. An open house is held every Saturday afternoon. Andrew really knows how to conduct a brewery tour—he says beer samples are given before, during, and after the tour.

THE BREWS

Andrew brews on a seven-barrel system purchased from a company in Miami, Florida, which had been unsuccessful in opening a brewery there. He uses nine different kinds of domestic malts, which are milled in house, and several kinds of domestic hops as well as Saaz from the Czech Republic. The beers are unfiltered. In 1994, he produced 311 barrels.

The beers are distributed in much of northern California in kegs and twenty-two-ounce bottles. Seasonals are distributed in sixteen-ounce bottles, all of which can be purchased at the brewery.

Etna Export Lager (1.050) is hazy gold with a fruity aroma and a short, light fruity, malty palate. Etna Dark Lager (1.048) is dark brown with a ruby hue and a tall, creamy, brown head; it has a smooth and light-bodied palate of deeply roasted malts, very lightly bittered. Etna Ale (1.048) is bright gold to amber with a fresh hay aroma and a fruity, malty palate with a slightly sour tang at the end. Etna Whiskey Butte Porter is dark nut brown with a tall brown head, a dry malt aroma, and a rich, deeply roasted malt palate with a nutty character. All of the beers tend to be fairly short, with little or no aftertaste. An Etna Weizen (1.038), Etna Bock, and Oktoberfest are produced seasonally.

LOST COAST BREWERY & CAFÉ

617 4th Street, Eureka, 95501

TELEPHONE: RESTAURANT, (707) 445-4480; BREWERY, 445-4484
DIRECTIONS: ON THE END OF EUREKA'S OLD TOWN SHOPPING DISTRICT. SOUTHBOUND ON HWY 101, BETWEEN G AND H STREETS
HOURS: DAILY: 11A.M.–1A.M.
SMOKING: NONE
ENTERTAINMENT: TV, HONKY TONK PIANO, DARTS, PINBALL, POOL
TOURS: BY APPOINTMENT
CREDIT CARDS: MASTERCARD, VISA

After visiting the enthralling wild surf, rock-studded beaches, and high cliffs of northern California's "lost coast" north of Cape Mendocino, where do you go for a bit of history and a bite to eat? Eureka! Lost Coast Brewery & Café is one of the greatest finds in California.

Barbara Groom and Wendy Pound started off the last decade of the 20th century by purchasing the former home of the Knights of Pythias. Nearly a year later, having brought the 1892 structure up to earthquake and local building codes (staying within the confines of the State Historic Codes), their turn-of-the-century saloon was ready for business. In so doing, they became the first women to build and operate a brewery in America.

Located on the edge of Eureka's Old Town shopping district, it has become a favorite of tourists and locals alike. Warm and welcoming, the dark-green facade is set off by antique carriage lamps. The interior boasts a copper-topped bar, wood floor, and high ceilings with antique fans. Wood-paneled walls display locally painted renditions of historic beer signs. Other colorful displays include collections of turbans, T-shirts, and beer coasters. The balcony is white and trimmed in dark wood with copper inserts. A must-see is the piano—the *copper* piano. On the main floor are the bar, family-style seating, and a pool room with a view of the entire brewing operation. Additional seating is available on the mezzanine level.

Wherever you choose to relax, be sure to check out the excellent pub-style menu which offers such delicacies as taquitos, nachos, and spicy hot Buffalo wings—and those are just appetizers! Try Lost Coast Stout Beef Stew—a hearty bowl with tender chunks of roast beef in a rich, dark stout gravy. Also wonderful is the tacos chicken salad, with chili beans, cheese, lettuce, salsa, and sour cream topped with strips of grilled chicken breast, all in a crispy tortilla bowl. They offer sandwiches for every taste and a build-your-own burger, which starts with a charbroiled hamburger, tofu burger or garden burger. For the wee ones, there is a children's menu. Note that the kitchen closes an hour before the bar.

THE BREWS

Demand from other bars and restaurants for Lost Coast brews has been so great that the brewery had to move to more spacious quarters down the street. The brewing is done by brewmaster and co-owner Barbara Groom and her assistant, Eric Sorensen. They are brewing with a ten-barrel brewhouse, which seems very small now compared to the thirty- and sixty-barrel fermenters they use in addition to the original ten-barrel tanks.

The brews are made with a base of American two-row pale malt to which they add imported specialty malts, all of which are milled in house. Domestic pellet hops are used and some of the brews are dry hopped. The pale ale, amber, and Downtown Brown are filtered; the other brands are generally not. In 1994, approximately two thousand barrels were produced.

Beers are available in twelve-ounce ($2.00) and pint ($2.50) servings. Some of the specialty brews are slightly more expensive. Samplers are sold individually in two- and four-ounce servings for 50¢ and 75¢. Gallon beer boxes, twenty-two-ounce bottles, and kegs and pony kegs are available for take out. Five to nine house beers are on tap at all times. In addition, they always have Guinness and one rotating micro on tap.

The lightest beer on tap is Lost Coast Harvest Wheat (1.050)—light maltiness and refreshing with very little bitterness. Downtown Brown (1.050) is an authentic tasting English brown—slightly sweet with roasted malts and very light hops and a soft mouth; it's a very pleasant session beer (a good beer to drink when drinking a lot; bronze 1993 GABF). Lost Coast Amber (1.054) has a beautiful, bright, reddish-copper color and a fruity roasted malt aroma; it's malty on the palate with light hops, and is very fresh and drinkable. Lost Coast Pale Ale (1.054) is bright gold with a yeasty-fruity aroma and a fresh hoppy flavor. Lost Coast Stout (1.064) is black with a brown head; it has a roasted barley, coffee aroma, a sweet entry, and delicious, bittersweet, espressolike finish. Other rotating brews include Apricot Wheat (1.050), Raspberry Brown, Pound's Porter, Oktoberfest, Irish Red, and XXX.

North Coast Brewing Co.

444 North Main, Fort Bragg, 95437

TELEPHONE: PUB, (707) 964-3400; BREWERY, 964-2739; FAX, 964-8768
DIRECTIONS: IT IS ON THE EAST SIDE OF HWY 1, ON THE CORNER OF PINE & MAIN, IN THE DOWNTOWN
HOURS: TUES–SAT: 2P.M.–11P.M.; CLOSED SUN & MON
WHEELCHAIR ACCESS: YES
SMOKING: NONE
ENTERTAINMENT: LIVE JAZZ SAT NIGHTS, TV, DARTS
TOURS: TUES–FRI AT 3P.M. & SAT AT 1:30P.M.; LARGE GROUPS SHOULD CALL BREWERY FOR AN APPOINTMENT
CREDIT CARDS: DISCOVER, MASTERCARD, VISA

North Coast Brewing offers many delights to the thirsty beer tourist. First is the wonderful beer. Then there is the delightfully tasty pub cuisine—and the beer. Then there is the welcoming and friendly staff—and the beer. Next is the charming English pub atmosphere—and the beer. And finally, quaint and interesting decor . . . and, oh yes, the beer. In case you haven't noticed, I am especially fond of . . . well, you get the picture.

North Coast Brewing in Fort Bragg is close enough to the ocean to boast a taste of salty air. In the path of the famous scenic route, Highway 1, the area offers views of orchards, wineries, redwoods, and ocean. Across the street, and behind the new North Coast microbrewing facility, is the Skunk railroad, offering tours to Willets, farther inland, along the old logging trail. In its earlier days,

North Coast Brewing's 1916 Victorian building was a mortuary, but there is nothing somber about it today.

The antique bar was rescued from an old Eureka saloon and is complemented by wood floors, tables, and chairs, with booths offering a modicum of privacy. The decor includes the Union Jack hanging from one wall, numerous pictures of North Coast logging in early days, ceiling fans, and a scattered collection of beer bottles.

The brewery can be viewed through multipaned windows, or for a better view, you can stroll down the back hall and view each stage of the brew process through a series of windows. The fireplace invites you to sit awhile.

The menu extends the invitation. For an experience ranging from the sophisticated to the just-for-fun, there is nothing like North Coast's appetizers. Sample the North Coast ceviche (made with bay scallops in a tangy onion, tomato, and cilantro marinade), the hush puppies with garlicky aioli, or the killer nachos.

The entrees present you with a delightful if problematic range of choices. Aside from the tempting nightly specials, described in the most delicious terms, there are beer-soused barbecue spareribs served with black beans, blackened Pacific red snapper, and sauteed cajun prawns with garlic, spices and a splash of Scrimshaw Pilsner. For the pasta lover there is seafood linguine, with scallops, prawns, and clams in a light herb butter, or angel hair pasta *aglio e olio*.

For more traditional pub fare try the burgers or the fish and chips. There is also chili, Cajun black beans, and dirty rice (a clean shot to immortality). Of course, no visit to this restaurant would be complete without sampling Mrs. Buford Neff's fruit cobbler or the chocolate Mendocino mud cake. Alas, the menu suggests you ask your server about dessert *specials*, which could cause second thoughts . . . and third thoughts. . . .

Whether you find yourself in Fort Bragg and hungry, or want a destination worth the drive, North Coast Brewing Company is perfect place for a relaxing meal . . . and, well, a beer.

THE BREWS

Master brewer Mark Ruedrich first took up homebrewing while living in Devon, England, in the 1970s. It was in Devon that he also developed an appreciation for traditional English ales. Mark opened the brewpub in 1988 with a seven-barrel brewhouse manufactured by a local boat-building company. Reconditioned Grundy tanks were used for fermenting and conditioning tanks. A new brewery was opened across the street at the end of 1994. The new brewhouse is sixty barrels in size and the fermenters are twice that big. The old brewery is still used as a pilot brewery to develop new products.

Mark uses all domestic malts, milled at the brewery. Domestic pellet or leaf hops are almost always used. Finishing hops are put in the whirlpool. All but the Blue Star are filtered. The brewery produced fifteen hundred barrels in 1994.

The beers are available in ten-ounce servings ($1.90), pints ($2.75), and pitchers ($7.50). Sampler sets sell for $3.50 for four, $4.25 for five. Beer is available for take out in six-packs.

Alt Nouveau (1.047) has a hazy, light copper to orange look, a fresh floral aroma, and a complex, fresh, hoppy-floral-citrusy-spicy palate. The Scrimshaw Beer (1.045) is an ale brewed to taste like a Czech pilsner. It is brilliant gold with a sweet malty entry and a crisp, hoppy finish—clean and well balanced. Blue Star Wheat Beer (1.047) has a slightly hazy gold look and a clean, lemon palate. It is smooth and refreshing. Ruedrick's Red Seal Ale (1.056) is bright amber-copper with a fresh, hoppy aroma and a pronounced hoppy-malty palate with a delightful, long, hoppy, resiny-spicy finish. Old No. 38 Stout (1.057) is inky black with a light brown, dense, creamy head. The aroma is rich with deeply roasted malt and barley—wonderful just to look at and smell, but wait until you taste it! It has a very creamy mouth feel and a fantastic, rich, dry, roasted barley palate with a bitter, burnt malt finish. The Traditional Bock (available from February to April) is copper with an aroma of fresh apricots and peaches and a dry, fruity-malty palate backed by some hop bitterness. Centennial Ale (1.072, available from May to August) is a beautiful, dark gold liquid that seems to glow, topped with a tall, creamy head. The palate is dry with a complex balance of fresh hops and malts that masks the alcohol of this powerful ale. There is also a seasonal Oktoberfest Ale and a Christmas beer.

North Coast has taken several medals at the GABF: Scrimshaw took the gold in the lager-ale category in 1992 and the bronze in 1994; Old No. 38 took the bronze 1992 and 1994 and the silver in 1993; Alt Nouveau took the bronze in 1993; and Oktoberfest Ale took the silver in 1992 in the American brown ale category.

HUMES BREWING CO.
2775 Cavedale Road, Glen Ellen, 95442

TELEPHONE: (707) 935-0723
DIRECTIONS: OFF HWY 12, NORTH OF SONOMA (PLEASE CALL FOR MORE SPECIFIC DIRECTIONS)
TOURS: BY APPOINTMENT

Did you ever let a hobby get out of hand? That's what happened to Peter Humes, a chef by trade who dabbled in amateur wine and beer making. With the goal of making a beer that would be both healthy and taste better, in 1993 he began putting together a brewery that would produce beer made with organically grown ingredients. Using mostly converted dairy equipment, Peter constructed a six-barrel brewery in the barn behind his house. The beers were either hand kegged or hand bottled in used champagne bottles. Humes Brewing is a one-man show, with Peter making and packaging the beer, washing the bottles, and delivering the beer.

THE BREWS

With the zeal known only to American homebrewers, Peter has striven to take the German purity law (the Reinheitsgebot) one step further. Not only does he use only the four basic ingredients—malted barley, hops, water, and yeast—Peter strives to make his beers even purer, using certified organically grown malts and hops and natural artesian water. No pesticides or chemical fertilizers are used in the growing and packaging of the malt and hops—and they cost about twice as much as the nonorganic kind. The malts and hops are a combination of domestic and foreign varieties. Hop varieties include Pride of Ringwood, which are grown in Tasmania, and California Clusters, grown on a farm near Sacramento. Peter claims his are the only commercially produced beers made with California hops.

The beers are unfiltered and are either bottle-conditioned in returnable 1.5 liter and 375 milliliter bottles or sold through the beer market in kegs. In 1994, he produced two hundred barrels of beer.

Cavedale Ale has a cloudy, copper color and a tall, tight, off-white head. The aroma is of fresh strawberries with light malt in the background. Malty in the middle, it finishes long, tangy, and bitter. Peter says it undergoes a long, cold fermentation and is a cross in style between an abbey ale and an alt. The Steep Canyon Stout is jet black with a tall, brown head and a creamy top; it leaves good lace on the glass. The body is full and silky, and the palate is rich with deeply roasted malt and notes of chocolate and coffee, firmly balanced with fresh hops.

Peter also makes Jaipur Pale Ale (an IPA that is dry hopped), Honey Wheat Brew, and a nonalcoholic Ginger Beer.

MENDOCINO BREWING CO. & HOPLAND BREWERY, BREWPUB & BEER GARDEN

13351 Highway 101 South (P.O. Box 400), Hopland, 95449

TELEPHONE: RESTAURANT, (707) 744-1361; OFFICE, 744-1015; FAX, 744-1910
DIRECTIONS: LOCATED ON THE EAST SIDE OF HWY 101, IN THE CENTER OF TOWN
HOURS: MON–SUN: 11A.M.–10P.M.; FRI: TILL 11P.M.; SAT: TILL 1:30A.M.
WHEELCHAIR ACCESS: YES
SMOKING: YES
ENTERTAINMENT: LIVE MUSIC SAT NIGHT, TV, DARTS
TOURS: BY APPOINTMENT
CREDIT CARDS: MASTERCARD, VISA

When the Mendocino Brewing Co. opened its doors on August 14, 1983, it was the first brewpub to open in California since Prohibition, and only the second in the United States. Mendocino had close links with New Albion Brewing Co. in nearby Sonoma, the first craft brewery to open in California since Prohibition. General partner Michael Laybourn had been inspired by New Albion, and when it closed in late 1982, he was able to pick up not only some of the New Albion equipment but also two good people—brewers Don Barkley and Michael Lovett.

The Hopland Brewery Brewpub has become a popular spot with both locals and tourists alike. In the early days, when it was one of the only brewpubs in the nation, people driving along Highway 101 discovered good beer here and took with them as souvenirs the unusual-looking twenty-two-ounce bottles of Red Tail Ale.

The pub is housed in a quaint, hundred-year-old brick building that once served as a U.S. post office and later as the Hop Vine Saloon. As the name implies, Hopland was a hop-growing area for many years, attested to by the hop motifs on the stamped tin walls of the old saloon. The hop industry died in the 1950s due to climatic changes, and changing economic conditions led farmers to replant pears and grapes.

Hop vines still grow on the trellises over the rustic beer garden, as do grape vines. The picnic tables under the arbor are a delightful place to enjoy a beer on a warm day. From the tables you can see the rather beaten up, original brew kettle from the New Albion Brewery. There is also a sandbox for the kiddies.

The Hopland Brewery Brewpub is a family-style restaurant with a saloonlike ambiance. As you enter, you will likely find a few locals clad in cowboy boots and hats. The handsome bar is blonde oak and brass, and many of the walls are bare brick. Separated by archways are the main dining area, a separate room with dart boards, and a stage for live performances. On the far side is a very well-stocked gift shop, including beer for take out.

The menu is American cuisine: hot beer sausages, burgers, seafood, fresh salads, and vegetarian items. Check for daily specials. Several California wines are offered.

Celebrations are held three times each year at the brewpub. They are held on the Fourth of July, the second weekend of August for their anniversary celebration, and in late September or early October for Oktoberfest.

THE BREWS

Masterbrewer Don Barkley began brewing as a hobby at home in 1971. When the New Albion Brewing Co. opened in 1977 he went to work there and became head brewer. At the same time he attended brewing school at the University of California at Davis. Don's chief assistants are head brewer Christopher Schweitzer and production manager Ed Nichols.

They work with a brewery which has been added onto and modified several times. The brewhouse is twenty barrels in size and there is a great variety of fermenters, ranging in size from 30 to 110 barrels. Brewing is performed three times a day, five days a week. In 1994, they produced 13,600 barrels.

Don says they use all American malts, which are crushed on site. The beers are hopped with American leaf hops, primarily Cluster and Cascade. The one exception is the imported Saaz leaf hops, which are used in the Eye of the Hawk. A hopjack strainer is used to impart hop flavor and aroma to their beers. All the beers are filtered, with the exception of the Peregrine Pale Ale, which is served cask-conditioned, and some the seasonal brews.

They normally have four beers on tap and a fifth seasonal on occasion. Two-ounce samplers are available at two for 50¢. Beer is available to go in twelve-ounce and twenty-two-ounce bottles.

The beers are named after local birds, mostly raptors, and have award-winning label designs. Peregrine Pale Ale is bright gold with light malts and has a fresh, citrusy hop finish. It has a very clean, smooth palate.

Blue Heron Pale Ale (1.054) is hazy gold with a more pronounced hoppy-bitter character. There is a touch of fruit and sweet maltiness in the background. Red Tail Ale (1.054) is amber and has a firm, toasted malt palate with a long, hoppy-bitter finish. Ebony colored Black Hawk Stout (1.054) has an intense, roasted malt palate and a full body; it finishes bittersweet with notes of chocolate. Seasonal brews include Eye of the Hawk Select Ale (1.064, made especially for the Fourth of July, their anniversary celebration, and the annual Oktoberfest), Springtide Ale (a spiced ale), and Yuletide Porter.

DOWNTOWN JOE'S BREWERY & RESTAURANT
902 Main Street, Napa, 94559

TELEPHONE: (707) 258-2337; FAX, 258-8740
DIRECTIONS: AT THE CORNER OF 2ND AND MAIN, NEXT TO VETERANS MEMORIAL PARK AND THE NAPA RIVER
HOURS: DAILY: 8A.M.–2A.M.
WHEELCHAIR ACCESS: YES
SMOKING: ONLY IN DESIGNATED AREAS
ENTERTAINMENT: LIVE MUSIC ON TUES, THUR–SUN
TOURS: BY APPOINTMENT
CREDIT CARDS: AMEX, DINERS CLUB, DISCOVER, MASTERCARD, VISA

Is nothing sacred? Even Napa, the heartland of wine country, has been invaded by brewpubs. The culprit is Downtown Joe's. Although the name sounds plain, this is the best bar in the Napa area—at least that's what the local paper has proclaimed.

Downtown Joe's first opened in 1988 as Willett's Brewing by Chuck Willett Ankeny, the great-grandson of Theodore Hamm, founder of Hamm's Brewing Co. It was joined briefly by the Brown Street Brewery, just a few blocks away. Then in late 1993 Willett's was purchased by Napa natives Joe Peatman and Joe Ruffino. The two Joes redecorated, expanded the bar, and upgraded the menu, but fortunately they retained the services of Brian Hunt, brewer par excellence.

Housed in the historic Oberon Building built in 1894, Downtown Joe's sports a 1930s Art Deco tile facade and a cheerful beer garden with a view of the Veterans Memorial Park and the Napa River. The Victorian bar fronts on Main Street and is frequented by locals, tourists, and lawyers from the nearby courthouse. It is decorated with antiques and turn-of-the-century photographs. The L-shaped bar sports a fancy copper top. In the rear of the building is a modern, elevated dining room with carpets and picture windows looking out on the wooded banks of the Napa

River. Between the bar and dining areas sit the gleaming, solid copper brew kettles and the stainless-steel mash tun.

Downtown Joe's is one of the only brewpubs in northern California serving breakfast, making it a good place to begin a regional brew tour. A full breakfast is offered, and the showstopper is Joe's Special—scrambled beef, sausage, onions, peppers, mushrooms, spinach, and eggs, topped with Jack cheese and served with house potatoes and toast. Saturday and Sunday brunch is awesome, featuring several kinds of eggs Benedict, fried oysters, huevos rancheros, and a seafood omelette.

The lunch and dinner menu includes a broad selection of seafood appetizers, salads, pizzas, pastas, sandwiches, and entrees, such as seafood stew, prawns scallop brochette and smoked pork chops. There is also a menu of light alternatives for the health-conscious, a children's menu, and a list of Napa Valley wines.

THE BREWS

Brewer Brian Hunt makes beer about twice a week with a seven-barrel, solid copper brew kettle manufactured by the Paul Zaft Copperworks, formerly of San Francisco. He uses primarily American malts and pellet hops. Beers are unfiltered and frequently served cask-conditioned. Production in 1994 was just under six hundred barrels. Beers are available in ten-ounce ($2.00) and sixteen-ounce servings ($3.00) and pitchers ($9.00). Prices are reduced during happy hour. Usually about six beers are on tap at a time. For take out there are 2.25-gallon party pigs and 5- to 15.5-gallon kegs.

Brian's first and lightest beer is Lickity Split Lager—gold, hazy, and undistinguished. Ace High Cream Ale is a zesty brew with a long, bitter-hoppy finish. Tail Waggin' Ale really will make your tail wag with a robust roasted malt and hop balance and a dry finish. Past Due Dark Ale is an American brown ale with a reddish-brown color and lots of roasted maltyness. It has a dry roasted malty and hoppy finish and is very drinkable. Summertime Wheat Beer is deep, cloudy gold with a sweet, malty palate. Golden Thistle Bitter bursts with flavor and complexity, beginning with an appetizing, fresh, hoppy aroma and ending with a long, satisfying bitter finish. In addition, Brian makes Specter of Worthy Stout for St. Patrick's Day and Halloween and a Christmas beer.

Brian is a real veteran of the American beer renaissance. For information on his background, read under Moonlight Brewing on p. 133.

NAPA VALLEY ALE WORKS

110 Camino Oruga (P.O. Box 5906), Napa, 94581

TELEPHONE: (707) 257-8381;
FAX, 257-2436
DIRECTIONS: ABOUT FIVE MILES SOUTH OF NAPA NEAR THE NAPA AIRPORT. GOING SOUTH ON ROUTE 29, JUST BEFORE REACHING ROUTE 12, TURN LEFT ON NORTH KELLY ROAD, THEN RIGHT ON CAMINO ORUGA
TOURS: BY APPOINTMENT

The Napa Valley Ale Works is unusual because it is the only brewery in the country using winemaking equipment in the brewhouse. Perhaps this should be expected when both partners have winemaking backgrounds. President John Wright was the founder and, until recently, the owner of Domaine Chandon. Brewmaster Elaine St. Clair studied both winemaking and beermaking at the University of California at Davis and is currently an assistant winemaker at Domaine Chandon. Her interest in beer, particularly Scottish ales, began in the home of her parents, who were born and raised in Scotland.

Elaine started brewing at home with her partner, Dwayne Mathews, back in 1988. In 1989 Elaine and Dwayne contracted with Anderson Valley Brewing Co. to make two ales. In 1994 they acquired their current building, which used to be an old Caterpillar parts warehouse. The first batch was made in May of the same year.

THE BREWS

The equipment for the Napa Valley Ale Works was acquired from a variety of sources. The most interesting and innovative, however, is the forty-barrel mash tun. Originally designed to ferment red wine, it is a horizontal, stainless-steel cylinder that rotates like a cement mixer. Blades inside the tank mix the grist. The mash is performed over a four- to five-hour period, more than double the time at other breweries.

Their two products are Red Ale (1.059) and Wheat Ale (1.048). John says they avoided the trend of naming beers after "dogs, fish, or people." Both beers are made with a base of North American two-row pale malt. The Red also has American crystal and a touch of Vienna malt. It is hopped with Cascades for bittering and American Tettnang for flavoring. In addition, it is dry hopped with Tettnangs for aroma. The wheat is made with malted barley and malted wheat at a seven-to-three ratio. It is bittered with American Tettnang and flavored with American Hallertau hops.

Napa Valley ales are available at the brewery in kegs, five-gallon canisters, and twenty-two-ounce and twelve-ounce bottles. The beers are sold throughout California.

Dempsey's Ale House & Sonoma Brewing Co.

50 East Washington Street, Petaluma, 94952

TELEPHONE: (707) 765-9694
DIRECTIONS: From Hwy 101, take the Washington Street exit; head west toward downtown Petaluma; it's in the Golden Eagle Shopping Center
HOURS: Daily: 11:30a.m.–10p.m.
WHEELCHAIR ACCESS: Yes
SMOKING: No smoking inside
TOURS: By appointment
CREDIT CARDS: MasterCard, Visa

Whether you call it Dempsey's Ale House or Sonoma Brewing Company, or like the sound of all those words rolling off your tongue together, this is the place in Petaluma for a unique dining experience. Where else can you have good food and beer, and dine at the edge of the Petaluma River? Petaluma began as an old hunting retreat, did a stint as the chicken capital of the world, and is now a nice little town with plans to stay that way. Dempsey's is located in the back of the Golden Eagle Shopping Center. From the windows there is a view of the river, or you can sit in the patio close to the foot bridge—as close as you can get to the river and still stay dry. Or tie up at the municipal marina and come ashore for a bite and a brew.

As you walk into Dempsey's, the first thing you notice are the red French doors offering a clear view of the brew tanks. The restaurant has decorative tile floors, ceiling fans, and hanging lights. Dempsey's is a popular place, and the atmosphere is casual with an eclectic mixture of patrons. The back bar is a beautiful and unusual mirrored, Art Deco piece from Willett's Brewery in Napa.

The menu continues the unique theme. It is constantly changing, according to seasonal foods and the inspiration of Bernadette Burrell, the chef and co-owner. Bernadette makes her own ketchup and mayonnaise and preserves her own olives and pickles. It doesn't get much fresher—or special—than that!

Dempsey's Food To Go is good to go. Their roasted garlic with focaccia and quesadilla with chiles and grilled onions are delicious, whether dining in or taking out. They also offer cheeseburgers, grilled pork chops and roasted chicken. Their menu offers international selections, featuring Southwestern, Italian, and California-style dishes such as red bean chili with cured sirloin or Thai curry mussel stew. There are pasta, fresh seafood, grilled meats, and homemade desserts, like the smooth, creamy Kahlua flan.

THE BREWS

While Bernadette reigns in the kitchen, husband Peter Burrell's realm is the brewery. Peter, a graduate of the Siebel Institute, was brewmaster at Squatter's Pub Brewery in Salt Lake City, Utah, and also worked at Sieben's in Chicago, Illinois, and Pearl Brewing in San Antonio, Texas.

Peter is making his beers with a fifteen-barrel system manufactured by JV Northwest. He uses domestic, two-row pale malts and primarily British specialty malts, milled on site. Mostly domestic pellet hops are used, but he does dry hop the bitter with Kent Goldings. His dunkelweizen and the strong ale are also dry hopped. The beers are filtered, with the exception of the stout, dunkelweizen and the strong ale. In 1994 Peter produced about seven hundred barrels.

The beers are available in servings of ten ounces ($2.00), sixteen ounces ($2.75), twenty-five-ounce schooners ($4.00), and pitchers ($7.75). Three-ounce samplers cost 75¢. Beer is available for take out in gallon cubes, 2.25-gallon party pigs, and 3-, 5-, and 15-gallon kegs. Usually about five beers are on tap at a time.

Golden Eagle Ale (1.048) is bright gold with a light malty aroma, and a perfumy-tangy palate with notes of licorice and a hoppy finish. Red Rooster Ale (1.054) is bright copper with a malty aroma and a medicinal, malty palate with a hint of licorice. Dunkelweizen is slightly hazy copper with a tangy herbal nose, a medicinal licorice palate, and a bitter, hoppy finish. Ugly Dog Stout (1.064) is dark brown to black with a heavy roasted malt palate and notes of coffee and licorice, a long, bitter finish, and a full, almost syrupy body (gold 1993 GABF).

Other beers include Petaluma Strong Ale, Bitter (served in the spring), Sonoma Irish Ale (1.050, served in the spring, gold 1992, bronze 1993 GABF), Noche Buena Barleywine (served at Christmas), Bad Bear Brown Ale, and Riverside Wheat (served in the summer).

LAGUNITAS BREWING CO.
1322 Ross, Petaluma 94954

> **TELEPHONE:** (415) 488-1601
> **DIRECTIONS:** CALL FOR DIRECTIONS
> **TOURS:** BY APPOINTMENT

Tony McGee's story is one that has occurred again and again—a homebrewer gone berserk. Tony says he started just cooking away on the stove. Five-gallon batches quickly grew to ten gallons, then twenty gallons, then thirty-one. Friends told Tony his beer was terrific, and before you knew it, he was applying for a brewery license.

It started in Lagunitas, one of those California drop-out spots on the coast north of San Francisco. In February of 1994, Tony started with a patched-together, seven-barrel system. But the brewery soon outstripped the plumbing system's capacity to handle the effluent. The operation moved to Petaluma at the end of the year, where a new, fourteen-barrel system was installed.

THE BREWS

Lagunitas beers are made with American pale malts and specialty malts from Britain. Willamette and Liberty pellet hops are used. Scott Wittenbaler, originally a homebrewer from Lagunitas who started helping Tony, is now the head brewer. Although production in 1994 was only 350 barrels, it has increased rapidly since the move to Petaluma. In June, they began packaging in twenty-two-ounce bottles.

You might have tried one of the Lagunitas beers and not even known it, since Tony brews mostly private-label beers for bars and restaurants in Marin County and throughout the Bay Area. Their three beers are Lagunitas Red, Dog House Ale, and Capuccino Stout. Unfortunately, I have yet to try the Lagunitas brews.

SANTA ROSA BREWING CO.
458 B Street, Santa Rosa, 95401

TELEPHONE: (707) 544-HOPS
DIRECTIONS: GOING NORTH ON HWY 101, TAKE THE DOWNTOWN SANTA ROSA EXIT, TURN RIGHT ON 3RD STREET AND LEFT ON B STREET. IT'S AT THE CORNER OF B AND 7TH STREETS IN DOWNTOWN SANTA ROSA
HOURS: SUN–WED: 11:30A.M.–MIDNIGHT; THUR–SAT: TILL 1A.M.
WHEELCHAIR ACCESS: YES
SMOKING: NONE
ENTERTAINMENT: LIVE MUSIC (ROCK/BLUES/REGGAE) THUR–SAT NIGHTS
TOURS: BY APPOINTMENT
CREDIT CARDS: AMEX, DISCOVER, MASTERCARD, VISA

It is hard to believe that a truly pleasant brewpub awaits inside the inelegant, red-brick building on B Street known by locals as "the brickyard." Not only is it pleasant, it receives my vote as the most improved brewpub in northern California.

Santa Rosa Brewing was originally opened in 1987 by Bruce Kelm as Kelmer's Brewhouse. Kelm took an old video store and remodeled it into an English sports pub. It was dimly lit, had a "men only" atmosphere, and served beer that ranged from very good to just so-so. In 1993 Kelmer's changed hands and new owners Frank, Kevin, and Diana McCullough changed almost everything about the place—name, menu, beers, interior decoration, and theme. Now it has that California light-and-airy feel, an imaginative and varied menu, and some ales that are worth going out of your way for. It welcomes families and is completely nonsmoking.

Outside, the brewhouse is displayed through windows on the street level. Once inside, you face a long bar directly ahead, with a dining area to the left and archways to the right, beyond which is an area for playing darts as well as another dining area. Just in front of the bar is a unique, seven-foot-high, two-inch-thick mug of beer that bubbles constantly—it would make a nice but thin aquarium. The blond oak tables are provided with captain's chairs. The walls are cream colored, and the windows look out on the street. A few TV sets (kept either at very low volume or muted) hang from the ceiling.

Head chef Tony Sissa, a graduate of the California Culinary Academy, makes a great variety of fresh dishes and incorporates house beers in several of the items, including the bread, pizza dough, steamed clams, and the fish and chips. The menu features several starters, including hot wings, a quesadilla, Sonoma coast crab cakes, fresh clams, and calamari. There are at least five different salad entrees and a variety of sandwiches and burgers. This is rounded out with gourmet pizza and calzones, soups, desserts, California wines, and a children's menu. Tony says the most popular item is the fish and chips, made with Icelandic pollock. All items are reasonably priced.

THE BREWS

Brewing is done by owner Frank McCullough and partner Tim O'Day. Tim came from England in 1987 to become partner and head brewer at Kelmer's. Tim took a bronze and a silver medal for his brews at the 1990 GABF. They started with a traditional, English-made, eight-barrel system with open fermenters and have since added one closed, sixteen-barrel fermenter. The beers are hopped with a combination of American and English pellet and leaf hops. Many of the beers are dry hopped, either in the fermenter or in the conditioning tank. The beers were originally in the traditional English style. Since reopening, Frank and Tim have tried about a dozen different yeasts and have experimented continuously (venturing as far afield as a Belgian wit beer, a spiced Christmas beer, and fruit beers using crushed whole fruit). Generally, a portion of each batch is filtered and combined back with the original batch. In this way the beer is clarified to some extent but is kept as alive as possible by the unfiltered portion. Production in 1994 was just under a thousand barrels. Beers are available in ten-ounce ($2.00), sixteen-ounce ($2.50), and twenty-three-ounce ($3.25) servings, and pitchers ($8.00). The brewmaster's special is priced slightly higher. Generally, four beers are on tap at a time. In addition, four guest beers are offered. Four five-ounce samplers are available for $3.00. For take out there are one-gallon containers and 5- to 15.5-gallon kegs. Some of Santa Rosa Brewing's beers are distributed to tap bars and brewpubs in the Bay Area.

Santa Rosa's two regular beers are Golden Pale Ale (1.052) and Two Rock Amber (1.058). Golden Pale Ale is deep gold with a fresh malty aroma and a hoppy palate; it is well balanced and dry. Two Rock Amber (1.060) has a beautiful, bright copper color, a complex aroma, and a delicious, deeply roasted malt palate with a crisp yet malty finish. The two other beers on tap, usually a porter or a stout, rotate. The Chocolate Porter is deep brown with a reddish tint and a creamy brown head. It has a dry, deeply roasted malt-coffee palate and is both nutty and burnt, with a hint of chocolate. Other beers are the Santa Rosa Amber Weizen (1.050, hazy copper with a soft, sweet malt character), Chinooky-nook (an IPA that is dry hopped with Chinook hops), Cascade IPA, and Santa Rosa Red (dry hopped with Chinook, Cascade, and Centennial). All of these are a hop lover's dream, with long, dry, fresh hoppy palates.

MOONLIGHT BREWING CO.
Windsor [Mailing address: P. O. Box 316, Fulton, CA 95439]

TELEPHONE: (707) 528-2537
TOURS: TOURS ARE NOT OFFERED AT THIS TIME

Brian Hunt's love affair with beer goes back to his high school days in Sacramento when he and a friend would sneak out to the garage and "ferment any living thing." He learned to take a more scientific approach while studying brewing at the University of California at Davis. Upon graduation in 1980, Brian went to work for Schlitz in Milwaukee. Whenever he had free time he used to wander around the old cellars filled with wooden tanks and open ferementers. Then, in 1981, Schlitz closed and Brian lost his job. Shortly after that he discovered the magic of ales while attending the Great British Beer Festival.

Brian returned to California and experienced a series of brewing misadventures. First, he worked on a project to open a brewery in Berkeley, which failed due to lack of capital, and then he worked for the Xcelsior Brewery in Santa Rosa. Finally, in 1987, things clicked—Brian landed the job as head brewer at the new Willett's Brewing Co. (now Downtown Joe's) in Napa. About the same time, he served as a consulting brewer for the start-up of Anderson Valley Brewing.

Being a scavenger at heart, Brian had collected bits and pieces from different breweries over the years, and in September, 1992, he opened his own brewery in the barn behind his house (which, ironically, sits in the middle of a vineyard). He guesses that up to fifteen different breweries are represented in different pieces of his brewing equipment, including the original malt mill from the New Albion Brewing Co.

Brewing four or more times a week between the two breweries, Brian brews at odd hours at home, hence the name "Moonlight" Brewing. Beer tourists are advised to stay away from the brewery due to Brian's hectic schedule and the cramped quarters in the brewery. You would be better off visiting one of the pubs that carries Brian's beers, such as Gaffney's on Mendocino Avenue in Santa Rosa or the Inn of the Beginning on the Old Redwood Highway in Cotati.

THE BREWS
Brian brews on a seven-barrel system about twice a week, with production running around five hundred barrels a year. He uses well water, does not filter his beers, and packages all of them in kegs.

Brian jokingly says he likes to make beers with so much character that they can only be appreciated by a small cadre of hardened beer lovers. Otherwise, his beers might become too popular, thereby requiring him to work harder. True, some of his beers are robust, but others are very soft, such as his Trick-or-Treat Ale (fruity, malty, and mellow) and the Fruit Medley (very fruity, smooth, and drinkable), which, by the way, has no fruit in it. Brian has a strong aversion to putting fruit in beer. One of Brian's most interesting beers is Old Combine 4-Grain: made with oats, rye, wheat, and barley, it has a soft, earthy character, with an indescribable something special to it. The Moonlight Pale Lager is aged for five or six weeks and has a fresh hoppiness, a good malt hop blend, and is immensely drinkable.

His more robust beers include Death-and-Taxes Black Beer (a black lager with rich coffee notes), Twist-of-Fate Bitter Ale (with a sharp hop palate and a long Cascade finish), and finally Bombay-by-Boat India Pale Ale—I didn't sample the latter, but guess that Brian would hop up an IPA pretty well. As you can tell, not only does Brian put character in his beers, but in their names as well.

Sacramento Valley and the Sierra

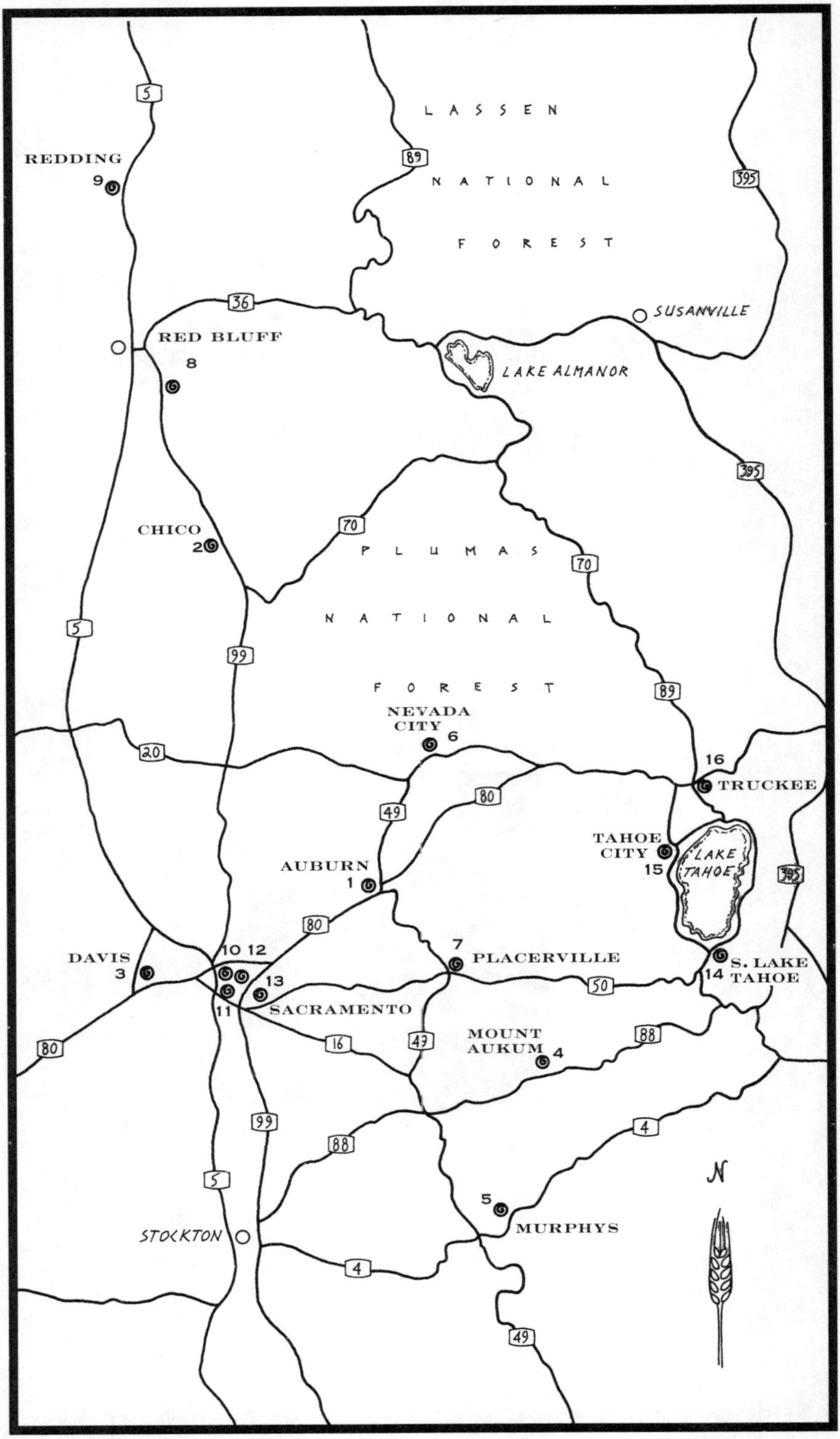
LASSEN NATIONAL FOREST
PLUMAS NATIONAL FOREST
REDDING 9
RED BLUFF 8
CHICO 2
SUSANVILLE
LAKE ALMANOR
NEVADA CITY 6
16 TRUCKEE
TAHOE CITY 15
LAKE TAHOE
AUBURN 1
DAVIS 3
10 12
11
13
SACRAMENTO
7 PLACERVILLE
14 S. LAKE TAHOE
MOUNT AUKUM 4
5 MURPHYS
STOCKTON
N
5
89
395
36
70
99
20
80
49
50
16
47
88
4

SACRAMENTO VALLEY AND THE SIERRA

City	Brewery (Map Key)	Page
Auburn	American River Brewing Co. (1)	138
Chico	Sierra Nevada Brewing Taproom & Restaurant (2)	139
Davis	Sudwerk Privatbrauerei Hübsch (3)	142
Mount Aukum	El Dorado Brewing Co. (4)	144
Murphys	Murphys Creek Brewing Co. (5)	145
Nevada City	Nevada City Brewing Co. (6)	146
Placerville	Hangtown Brewery (7)	147
Red Bluff	Tuscan Brewing Co. (8)	149
Redding	Red, White & Brew (9)	150
Sacramento	Hogshead Brewpub (10)	152
	River City Brewing Co. (11)	154
	Rubicon Brewing Co. (12)	156
	Sutter Brewing Co. (13)	158
South Lake Tahoe	Brewery at Lake Tahoe (14)	159
Tahoe City	Blue Water Brewing Co. (15)	161
Truckee	Truckee Brewing Co. & Pizza Junction (16)	163

American River Brewing Co.

100 Borland Avenue, Auburn, 95603

TELEPHONE: (916) 889-0841
DIRECTIONS: FROM I-80, TAKE THE ELM AVENUE EXIT; WHERE HIGHWAY 49 ENTERS THE AMERICAN RIVER CANYON
TOURS: SAT 9A.M.–5P.M.

For eight years American River Brewing was little more than a dream. In 1985 Don Smith and Jim Fair, engineers in Silicon Valley, fell in love with craft beer. They began making beer at home, with the idea that some day they would move out of the urban rat race to a small town where they could set up their own brewery. By 1991 Don and Jim had a business plan, had raised enough capital, and had hooked up with another beer enthusiast, John Mehohass.

Family ties led the partners to Auburn. It was just a few miles from here, on the American River, that gold was first discovered in California, and thousands flocked here to seek their fortunes. It seemed only natural that they should name their brewery after the river.

The partners built their own 8.5-barrel brewhouse. For fermenters, they have both thirty- and sixty-barrel tanks made from dairy equipment. To fill one of the small fermenters, they have to brew three consecutive batches. In November 1993 their first beer was distributed. In 1994, they produced eight hundred barrels.

THE BREWS

All three American River beers are made with all domestic two-row pale and specialty malts, milled at the brewery. Both leaf and pellet domestic hops are used. All of the beers are filtered before packaging, and they are distributed in both twelve-ounce bottles and kegs, which can be purchased at the brewery. American River beers are distributed from the Central Valley to Lake Tahoe.

American River Gold Lager (1.054) has a very clean palate with light hops and malt. The Amber Lager (1.056) is light copper with a smooth, roasted-malt palate. American River Stout (1.067), an oatmeal stout, is dark brown with a light brown head and a complex palate of sweet roasted malt and a bitter, slightly tart finish.

SIERRA NEVADA BREWING TAPROOM & RESTAURANT

1075 East 20th Street, Chico, 95928

TELEPHONE: RESTAURANT, (916) 345-2739; BREWERY, 893-3520; FAX, 893-8748
DIRECTIONS: FROM HWY. 99, TAKE THE 20TH STREET EXIT AND GO WEST (AWAY FROM THE CHICO MALL)
HOURS: TUES–SAT: 11A.M.–11P.M.; SUN–10A.M.– 2P.M. (BRUNCH); CLOSED MONDAY
WHEELCHAIR ACCESS: YES
SMOKING: NONE
TOURS: TUES–FRI AT 2:30P.M.; SATURDAY FROM NOON–3P.M.; OR BY APPOINTMENT
PARKING: IN LOT (FREE)
CREDIT CARDS: MASTERCARD, VISA

Sierra Nevada has grown from humble beginnings to become the largest craft brewery in the United States and one of the most respected breweries in the world. Ken Grossman and Paul Camusi are the geniuses and driving force behind Sierra Nevada. Like the Wright brothers, they started out tinkering with bicycles. While the Wright brothers invented human flight, Ken and Paul (re)invented beer.

In 1978, inspired by their exposure to homebrewing and the opening of New Albion Brewing in Sonoma, the pair began working on their own brewery. By early 1981, using family money, they produced their first bottle of Sierra Nevada Pale Ale. It has an unforgettable huge palate of Cascade hops. The original ten-barrel brewery was located on Gilman Street and put together with used equipment from old breweries, dairies, and creameries.

Because of Ken and Paul's uncompromising dedication to quality and flavor, Sierra Nevada beers have developed a loyal following. Their Porter and Stout quickly followed the Pale Ale and by the end of the year they produced their first holiday beer, Celebration Ale, which has become legendary. In 1985 they produced their first seasonal barleywine: Big Foot, a beer as husky as the creature who inspired its name. In 1990 Sierra Nevada produced its first lager: Pale Bock, which proved to many ale drinkers that lagers could be exciting too.

In 1989 the brewery moved to new quarters on 20th Street. The new facility features a pub and a showcase brewery with a hundred-barrel, solid-copper brewhouse purchased from the Bavarian Brewing Co. in Aschaffenberg, Germany.

The pub is tastefully decorated with tiled and carpeted floors, dark wood accents, and a classic mahogany back bar with stained glass and mirrors. The spectacular brewhouse can be seen through large windows in the restaurant. There is a pleasant beer garden with seating for fifty on one side of the building.

The menu features imaginative appetizers, such as ginger clams, Buffalo wings, Cajun veggies, soups, and salads, and a variety of pub entrees such as burgers, fish and chips dipped in Pale Ale batter, and several sandwiches. There is a variety of entrees for dinner, including eggplant parmesan, fettucini, linguine, seafood, chicken, and several beef dishes. A children's menu is offered for the wee ones. They also offer a selection of northern California wines.

THE BREWS

As mentioned before, the beers are brewed in a hundred-barrel, solid copper kettle. From there, the wort is transferred into stainless-steel, square, open fermenters (the two lagers, Summerfest and Pale Bock, are fermented at colder temperatures in closed fermentation vessels). After several days the beer is transferred into closed-conditioning tanks. Demand has kept the place humming. In 1994, they produced 157,000 barrels. At this rate, they average more than four brews a day every single day of the year. The operation is overseen by brewmaster and company co-founder Ken Grossman and head brewer Steve Dresler.

A variety of American malts are used, including two-row pale, caramel, dextrin, chocolate, and black malts. All American leaf hops are used, including Centennial, Nugget, Perle, Willamette, Mount Hood, American Hallertauer, and lots of Cascades. The Celebration and the Big Foot brands are dry hopped. All of the brands are filtered except for the wheat. The bottled beers receive a tiny dosage of yeast and dextrin just before bottling.

The Tap Room normally has seven to ten beers on tap. They are available in half pints, pints, and pitchers. Prices range with the brand—half pints cost $1.25 to $2.50, pints $2.00 to $2.25, pitchers $6.25 to $6.95. Some brands are available in bottles. Sampler sets of two ounces each are available for $4.50. Take outs are available in six packs and cases. The beers in the Tap Room are frequently keg-conditioned, that is, served under natural CO_2 pressure.

Sierra Nevada Pale Ale (1.052) is amber with a fresh, fragrant Cascade hop aroma and a big, complex palate with heavy doses of malt followed by even bigger doses of fresh, resiny Cascade hops in the finish. It is both tangy and citric. The Pale Ale won the gold medal in its category at the GABF in 1987, 1989, 1990, 1992, and 1993. Sierra Nevada Draught Ale is a toned-down version of the Pale Ale—very drinkable, yet flavorful.

Sierra Nevada Porter (1.058, bronze 1987 GABF) is dark brown with complex, deeply roasted malt and citric hop aroma and a long, dry, complex, deeply roasted to burnt malt and fresh, hoppy palate. Sierra Nevada Stout (1.062, silver 1988, 1989 GABF) is dark brown with a rich and complex, hoppy-estery-malty aroma, a sweet, deeply roasted malt palate, and a sweet but drying finish of roasted barley with plenty of bitterness.

The beers that follow are available seasonally. Sierra Nevada Wheat (1.052) is cloudy gold with a pronounced, resiny, Cascade finish. Sierra Nevada Summerfest (1.046, silver 1991 GABF, European classic Pilsner category) is brilliant gold with a malty entry and a big, dry hoppy finish. Sierra Nevada Pale Bock (1.064) is deep gold with a tall head, a spicy-estery aroma, and a sweet, malty entry followed by a long, dry, and very bitter, hoppy finish—full bodied and a real lip smacker.

Celebration Ale (1.064) is an extremely big beer with an orange-copper color, a complex and pungent floral-hop aroma, and a very strong roasted malt character overshadowed by a hoppy-resiny, citrusy, piny and spicy character. It is very long and full bodied. Celebration won the bronze medal in the amber ale category at the 1990 GABF and the silver in the IPA category at the 1994 festival.

Bigfoot Barleywine Style Ale (1.092, gold 1988, 1992 GABF) is orangish copper with a complex, fruity-flowery-nutty-estery aroma. It hits your palate like a Mack truck, first with sweet malt, followed by rich, sweet, and nutty malt, alcohol, and lots of hoppy bitterness. It is extremely big and long.

Other brands include Crystal Wheat (1.052) and Brown Ale (gold 1987 GABF). The Pale Bock, Summerfest, Crystal Wheat and Brown Ale are only available on tap in the Chico area.

Sudwerk Privatbrauerei Hübsch

2001 Second Street, Davis, 95616

TELEPHONE: Brewery, (916) 756-2739; Restaurant, 758-8700; Fax, 753-0590
DIRECTIONS: From I-80, take the Mace Boulevard exit, head north and after two miles, go left on Second Street; it is on the corner of Pole Line Road and Second
HOURS: Mon–Wed: 11:30a.m.–midnight; Thur: till 12:30a.m.; Fri–Sat: 11a.m.–1a.m.; Sunday till midnight
WHEELCHAIR ACCESS: Yes
SMOKING: None
ENTERTAINMENT: Live music (jazz, rock, reggae, blues), pool, video, darts, pinball, foosball
TOURS: By appointment
PARKING: Off street (free)
CREDIT CARDS: Amex, MasterCard, Visa

Sudwerk is one of America's most authentic and impressive German brewery restaurants. Its unique blend of German and American beer, victuals, and atmosphere puts it near the top of my list of places to visit. The exterior is brick and wood. Just outside is a German-style beer garden offering patio dining in an elegant setting: wrought-iron furniture, potted plants, and carriage lamps under the California sky.

Inside is one of the most impressive brewhouse views in the country. The beautiful copper kettles are showcased in the very middle of the first room as you enter, with the bar completely circling it. The warm welcome from the beer garden is continued inside with parquet floors, a blonde oak bar, hanging flags, oak paneling, brass lighting, and a view of the open fermentation process behind windows. They even have unique entertainment, offering live Bavarian and jazz music.

Sudwerk's menus offer appetizers such as beer-batter onion rings, a sausage sampler, Cajun chicken wings, and calamari rings. The salads include something for everyone, from teriyaki chicken to vegetarian pasta. There is also a children's menu.

Worth mentioning are the sausages—all served with German potato salad and sauerkraut, of course. Chicken-apple sausage tempts your tastebuds and it's low-fat to boot (only about 340 calories). Nurenberger bratwurst is an authentic country-style German sausage featuring finely ground pork and marjoram. Andouille is a medium-hot port sausage using Cajun spices. Octoberfest is a delightful hickory-smoked pork and beef German bratwurst using Gerhard's Napa Valley sausage.

The lunch menu also offers Jaeger Schnitzel, a boneless piece of veal rolled in bread crumbs then sauteed and topped with mushroom gravy, and a pancake plate, a crispy fried German potato pancake served with your choice of one of their four sausages, applesauce, and blueberries.

For a lighter choice, there are lemon pepper chicken and teriyaki chicken sandwiches.

The dinner menu adds such choices as Kassler Rippchen, a juicy, freshly smoked pork loin chop, and Hungarian goulash, diced pork and beef sauteed with onions, peppers, and Hungarian spices, served over homemade spâtzle noodles. And of course, for a fitting end (even though nothing else will fit for a week), Chocolate Suicide: three layers of chocolate cake with fudge frosting between each layer, topped with a piece of chocolate and surrounded on the outside with chopped almonds.

Whatever you choose, you will enjoy the food, atmosphere, beverages, and music. Sudwerk is well worth going out of your way to visit.

THE BREWS

Sudwerk is German for "brew house." The beautiful copper brewhouse is the heart and soul of both the restaurant and the brewery. In 1988, Ron Broward and Dean Unger, the future architect and builder of Sudwerk, traveled to Germany looking for good beer, a good manufacturer of brewing equipment, and a good brewmaster. They found all three.

Brewmaster David Sipes was trained in brewing science at the University of California at Davis and worked under Sudwerk's original brewmaster, Karl Eden.

The brewery was manufactured in Bamberg, Germany by Schulz. It is fully automated and controlled by a computer terminal. It produces about thirteen barrels of wort in each batch. An infusion mash is typically used, but a decoction mash is used for the bock. Due to the hardness of Davis' water, it must be softened before it can be used for brewing. The wort is transferred to four open, square, stainless-steel fermenters. After initial fermentation, the beer is racked to twenty-five-barrel lagering tanks. The beers are unfiltered and most of the beer is bottled or kegged for sale at off-premise accounts. American and British malts are used predominantly, with German malts added on occasion. The hops are both pellet and leaf from the Pacific Northwest and Hallertau Mittelfrueh and Hersbrucker Tettnang from Germany. Aroma hops are added in the whirlpool for many of the beers. The beers are normally lagered for at least six weeks. In 1994, forty-seven hundred barrels were produced.

Usually, five beers are on tap—the Lager, Pilsner, Märzen, Hefeweizen, and a seasonal. They are served in two sizes: .3-liter ($2.00) and one-liter glasses ($4.75). Beer is available to go in twelve- and twenty-two-ounce bottles and kegs and pony kegs.

Hübsch Bräu Lager (gold 1994 GABF in the Munchner helles category) is bright gold-amber with a well-balanced, fresh, and tasty malt palate followed by a tangy hoppy finish. Hübsch Bräu Pilsner (silver 1991, 1993 GABF) is bright gold with a flowery nose and palate and a refreshing hop finish. Hübsch Bräu Märzen (bronze 1991 GABF) is clear copper with a very smooth sweet-malt entry, a complex, malty middle, and a tangy, dry finish. Hübsch Hefe Weizen is hazy gold with an exciting, yeasty, clovey aroma. The palate has a fresh, fruity, tart character with plenty of malt also. Hübsch Holiday Dopplebock is clear, dark brown with a reddish tint, a rich, deeply roasted malt aroma, and a sweet, roasted malt palate with a bittersweet toffee finish.

EL DORADO BREWING CO.

P.O. Box 3, Mount Aukum, 95656

TELEPHONE: (916) 620-4253
TOURS: BY APPOINTMENT ONLY—PLEASE CALL THE BREWERY FOR AN APPOINTMENT AND DIRECTIONS

The El Dorado Brewing Co. is located on the edge of the Eldorado National Forest on the western slope of the Sierra Nevada mountain range at an elevation of thirty-five hundred feet. The closest town, Mount Aukum, lies ten miles west of the brewery in El Dorado County, approximately half way between Lake Tahoe and Sacramento.

Owner/brewer Jim Boyer began this business in 1991 after achieving success as a homebrewer. For the next several years he accumulated his equipment and renovated the brewery building, a task made simple by virtue of Jim's experience as a general contractor.

After all the preparations, the brewer and brewery were finally ready in the summer of 1994. The brewhouse utilizes two eighty-gallon Groen kettles for the mash tuns, a ten-barrel kettle from The Pub, and six seven-barrel Grundy tanks for fermentation. While the twenty-two-ounce bottles are still filled by hand, a Meheen bottler fills the twelve-ounce bottles. The beer is available in the Sacramento-Stockton-Lake Tahoe triangle.

It may seem confusing, but there are two El Dorado Brewing Companies. The other one is a brewpub in Stockton.

THE BREWS

Jim's one product is called Real Mountain Ale, an IPA that he dry hops, fines, and bottles unfiltered. Real Mountain is a hop lover's delight, with a fresh hop aroma and a sharp, hoppy, spicy, resiny, and bitter palate with sweet malt to balance. A stout is due in the fall of 1995 as well as a spiced ale for the holiday season. Jim says he will eventually provide his beer in kegs as well.

MURPHYS CREEK BREWING CO.
Murphys Grade Road (P.O. Box 1076), Murphys, 95247

> **TELEPHONE:** (209) 736-BREW; FAX, 736-0207
> **DIRECTIONS:** GOING NORTHEAST FROM ANGELS CAMP ON HWY 49, TURN RIGHT ON MURPHYS GRADE; IT'S ABOUT TWO AND A HALF MILES AHEAD, ON YOUR LEFT
> **TOURS:** BY SPECIAL REQUEST; TASTING ROOM IS OPEN SAT AND SUN FROM 11A.M.–5P.M.

When the gold miners rushed to the foothills of the Sierra Nevadas in 1848 and 1849, breweries came right behind them. Austrians and Germans opened breweries in virtually every mining town in the Mother Lode, and two or more breweries in the larger towns. Murphys, the Queen of the Sierra, had two breweries as early as 1848: the Hauselt and Heiden (or Murphys) Brewery, located in Brewery Gulch (now the Black Sheep winery), and the Charles Anderson Brewery, located on north Main Street. Unfortunately, as the gold petered out, so did the breweries.

The brewing renaissance has seen the return of brewing to the Mother Lode, with breweries now operating in Murphys, Nevada City, Auburn, Placerville and Mount Aukum. Dan Ayala brought brewing back to Calaveras County when he opened his Murphys Creek Brewing Co. in May of 1993.

THE BREWS
Micah Millspaw, also a partner, is the brewmaster at Murphys Creek. Over the years, Micah, a longtime homebrewer, has won a whole wall full of ribbons and awards for his beers and meads. He brews with an eleven-barrel brewhouse that he and Dan put together themselves. The fermenters are twenty-five barrels, so they do consecutive brews to fill them. They have their own well for the brewery, and Micah says the water is excellent for brewing. He uses a combination of domestic and imported specialty malts, which he mills himself, as well as domestic pellet hops. The wort for each brew is strained through a hop back containing leaf hops, for added aroma and flavor. The Red, the Golden Wheat, and some of the specialty beers are dry hopped. All of the beers are filtered. The

beers are distributed in kegs and twenty-two- and twelve-ounce bottles throughout northern California and Colorado; these are also for sale at the brewery. In 1994, production reached twelve hundred barrels.

Golden Wheat Beer (1.045) is clear, pinkish amber with a light, medium-roasted malt palate and a lightly bitter finish (made with a fifty-fifty ratio of malted barley and wheat). Murphys Red Beer (1.050) is bright copper with a fruity-malty aroma, a fruity palate, a light, bitter finish, and a thin body. Black Gold Stout (1.057) is inky black with a tight, dark brown head, a deeply roasted and smoky malt aroma, and a deeply roasted malt palate with a dry, burnt finish.

Some of the specialty beers include Cherry Red, Raspberry, Black Bart (stout), Bitter Angels (IPA), Jüle (strong ale for Christmas), Murphys Bock, and Murphys Irish Ale (peat ale).

NEVADA CITY BREWING CO.

75 Bost Avenue, Nevada City, 95959

TELEPHONE: (916) 265-2446
DIRECTIONS: FROM HWY. 49, TAKE THE RIDGE ROAD EXIT; MAKE AN IMMEDIATE RIGHT ON SEARLS AVENUE AND TURN RIGHT ON BOST
TOURS: FRIDAY: 3–5P.M.; SATURDAY: 1–5P.M.

Gene Downing, a retired air force pilot, switched from flying to fermenting in 1986 when he helped his brother, Steve, open the Truckee Brewing Co. in nearby Truckee. Bitten by the brewing bug, he decided to open his own brewery. In 1989, with help from Steve and others, he did just that in an industrial section of Nevada City. In so doing, he reintroduced brewing to the Mother Lode. Many breweries had flourished in this area in the nineteenth century, but they had gradually died out. Since the opening of Nevada City Brewing, several breweries have opened in the area.

Although some people might think Nevada City is located in the state of Nevada, that's just too logical—it's in California. The city has boasted over a dozen breweries in its past, but Gene's brewery is the only one there now. Today, the city offers a delightful trip back in time, featuring old hotels, restored Victorian homes, museums, and antique stores. Be sure to visit Friday or Saturday afternoon; that way you can tour the brewery, a treat not be missed.

Nevada City Brewing is the closest thing to being a brewpub without actually being one. On your tour you will be greeted by a welcoming crew of brewery volunteers known as the "brewery rats"—they will patiently explain every phase of the operation (including the six fermenters, which they call "the largest six pack in the state of California"), show you their large collection of beer memorabilia (including thousands of bottles, neon signs, and tap handles), pour as much beer as you like, and play a game of darts with you. Beebe, the yellow rat cat and brewery mascot, will even pose for a snapshot. Now, how's that for hospitality! The beers are distributed throughout California.

Before you go, don't forget to load up on "brew happens" bumper stickers, T-shirts, and bottles of beer for take out in twelve-, twenty-two-, and fifty-ounce bottles.

THE BREWS

Gene brews with a system he designed and had manufactured by a company in Nevada City. It features one four-hundred-barrel mash tun and two two-hundred-barrel brew kettles, requiring each batch to be split in two. After the boil, the wort is recombined into a four-hundred-barrel primary fermenter. The kettle is heated with steam heat. American malts, milled at the brewery, are used, along with leaf Nugget and Mount Hood hops. The beers are unfiltered. About six hundred barrels were produced in 1994.

California Gold Lager is hazy gold with a smooth, refreshing palate. California Dark Lager is light brown with a light malt palate. California Stout Lager is a reddish brown with a nice roasted malt palate with light bitterness in the finish.

HANGTOWN BREWERY

560A Placerville Drive, Placerville, 95667

TELEPHONE: (916) 621-3999; FAX, 621-2157
DIRECTIONS: FROM HWY 50, TAKE THE PLACERVILLE DRIVE EXIT AND GO NORTH ABOUT 1.3 MILES; IT'S ON THE RIGHT
TOURS: MON–THUR: 10A.M.–7P.M.; FRI–SAT: TILL 8P.M.; SUN: NOON–5P.M.

Placerville is a living legend of the Mother Lode. In 1848, just eight miles north of here in Coloma, James Marshall made the first discovery of gold at Sutter's Mill. For about a year, the mining camp was known as Dry Diggin's because the miners had to cart the dry soil down to the nearest stream to wash it. The next year it became known as Hangtown, due to some grizzly lynchings. Hangman's Tree is still there and marked with a plaque. In 1854 the town changed its name to the less stigmatic Placerville. Today a movement is afoot to go back to the town's original name.

Hangtown quickly became the center for wagon and mail routes (the Pony Express ran through here), and later for the telegraph. For a couple of months it was even the state capital. Breweries popped up to help slake the thirst of the miners and camp followers. Several businessmen who later gained national prominence got their start here—Mark Hopkins was the grocer, Philip Armour was the butcher, and John Studebaker the wagonmaker. Levi Strauss got his start here before moving on to San Francisco.

Much of old Placerville is preserved today, which makes it a fascinating stopover on your tour of the Mother Lode. And don't forget to stop by one of the newest attractions, the Hangtown Brewery. One day, when David Coody gains national prominence as a brewer, you can say, "I was there when he got started."

THE BREWS

Brewer David Coody was an X-ray technologist who brewed at home for many years. When the brewing renaissance began, he compared his homebrew with the new craft beers and, as so many others have done, said, "Hey, I can do this." In December 1992, he began distributing his first beers.

David operates a twenty-barrel brewery that he built himself. He uses all American two-row pale malt and specialty malts, which he mills in house. Both domestic and imported pellet hops are used. All of the beers are filtered. They are distributed in twelve- and twenty-two-ounce bottles and kegs throughout most of northern California, and they can also be purchased at the brewery. In 1994 production reached five hundred barrels.

Placerville Pale Ale is a bright, deep gold with a complex aroma of fruit, malt, and fresh hops. The hops in the palate are tangy and very pronounced with a good mixture of malt and bitterness. Howlin' Brown Ale (1.042) is done in the English brown ale style. It has a dark brown color and a light brown head. The aroma is of rich, chocolate malt, and the palate begins sweet and malty and finishes with dry, deeply roasted malts and chocolate with medium bitterness to back it up. Other beers include Light Ale, Wheat, Placerville Stout (1.058), and Boysenberry (1.050).

Tuscan Brewing Co.

25009 Kauffman Avenue, Red Bluff, 96080

TELEPHONE: (916) 527-7048
DIRECTIONS: From Red Bluff, go south about six miles on Hwy 99E. Turn left on Kauffman, then cross two bridges. It's the second house on the right
TOURS: By appointment only

Craft breweries have popped up in some of the most unlikely places, and Tuscan Brewing is a good example. It is tucked away in a shed in a walnut orchard about six miles south of Red Bluff.

Owner/brewer Val Theis had been brewing at home for about ten years, working on his recipes and perfecting his brewing techniques, when he decided he might actually be able to make a living at his pastime. Being short on capital, he scrounged around and finally constructed a seven-barrel brewery using converted dairy equipment and used Grundies from England. The brewery is housed in a metal shed behind his house. His first batch of beer went out the door in 1993. For the first two years Val hand bottled and labeled his beers, but he has since purchased bottling and labeling equipment.

Beer may be purchased at the brewery by the case in twelve- and twenty-two-ounce bottles.

THE BREWS

Val makes three beers on a regular basis: Pale Ale, Amber Ale, and Stout. He brews twice a month on average, and produced about 160 barrels in 1994. He uses domestic and Munich malts. They are all hopped with leaf Cascades and German Hallertau. The latter are used in dry hopping. The beers are unfiltered and clarified with isinglass finings. The beers are distributed in the Red Bluff area in kegs and twenty-two ounce bottles.

The one beer I sampled was the Pale Ale (1.064). It has a slightly hazy gold to amber color. The palate starts out sweet and malty and finishes with a burst of fresh hops and fruity notes.

RED, WHITE & BREW

2181 Hill Top Drive, Redding 96002

TELEPHONE: (916) 222-5891;
FAX, 222-0553
DIRECTIONS: FROM I-5 NORTH, TAKE THE CYPRESS TREE EXIT; TAKE A LEFT ON HILL TOP DRIVE; IT'S ON THE RIGHT
HOURS: DAILY: 11A.M.–11P.M.
WHEELCHAIR ACCESS: YES
SMOKING: NONE
ENTERTAINMENT: DARTS
TOURS: DROP-IN BASIS
PARKING: OFF-STREET (FREE)
CREDIT CARDS: NONE

Hidden away in a cinder-block building on Hill Top Drive is a unique experience in brewpubs. It looks like just another place for a sandwich and a beer from the outside. But step through the carved oak doors and you'll find a fun place with lots of great food and original brews. Inside, the walls are made of sound-absorbing carpet in bright red and blue, and the ceilings are white. The bar, booths, benches, and the area behind the bar are made from pews from the Star of the Sea Church after it closed in the Santa Cruz Mountains. They are stained ash and lend an atmosphere of almost heavenly coziness. The cross-beams are made out of the kneelers from the church, and the piano came from a little church in Cyprus. They have dart boards hanging on the carpeted walls (making it easier to retrieve the darts if you miss the board!), or settle down to a game of checkers or chess. There are collections of framed beer posters and brass plates that add to the welcoming ambience.

Owners Bill Ward and Frank Chorney are two old navy buddies, hence the patriotic theme of their business. Friendly and affable guys, they provide a comfortable atmosphere for local farmers, professionals, and just plain folks. The music is mostly jazz and R&B. They are hoping to include a beer garden with barbecue.

Bill used to work for Lockheed in the Bay Area, where he frequented some of the brewpubs. When he suddenly found himself without a job, he decided to look into making a living from his favorite pastime, drinking beer. After attending business courses at a local college and brewing classes at at the University of California at Davis, he began looking for a location for a brewpub. After Bill saw people fishing in the Sacramento River as he drove over the bridge in Redding, he and Frank decided this was the place. The brewpub opened in June of 1993.

The menu is mostly "pub grub" with a political twist. You might try the Clinton, a turkey sandwich, or the Hillary, same sandwich without the turkey. If you are tired of turkey, there is the Ross Perot, a veggie sandwich (they might add squirrel meat—depending on availability).

For those who wish to increase their global awareness, there is the Al Gore, a dolphin-safe tuna sandwich. Some menu items are so politically incorrect that, well, let's just say you have to go and check it out for yourself! Of course they also have nonpolitical fries and onion rings, homemade chips and salsa, and an assortment of delicious sausages and deli-style sandwiches pretty much made to order.

The drive to Redding is worth the trip, especially with the beauty of Mount Shasta nearby. The food is good and the atmosphere is friendly—be prepared to laugh and have a great time.

THE BREWS

Bill found his equipment at a brewery that never quite managed to open—the Huttenhain's Brewing Co. in Benicia. The brewery consists of equipment obtained from different sources: a one-barrel mash tun; a one-barrel brewhouse that was originally a large soup kettle; ten fifty-five-gallon, closed, stainless-steel fermenters; one seven-barrel Grundy fermenter; and three seven-barrel serving tanks.

Domestic two-row pale and specialty malts are used, as well as domestic pellet hops. The beers are unfiltered. They are served in pints ($2.50) and pitchers ($7.95). Samplers are available. The beers rotate, with one to three beers on tap at any given time. Beer is available to go in one-liter, four-pint, and half-gallon containers. Homebrewing supplies are available for sale.

The Amber Beer (named after a waitress) is their best-seller. On my visit to the pub I sampled two beers: Veteran's Day Special (complete with a hand grenade on the tap handle) is bright gold with a slight floral aroma, sweet malt entry and middle and an interesting tangy-spicy hop finish; the Lassen Lava (a porter) is dark auburn with a sweet, licorice aroma and a buttery, malty, and licorice palate.

HOGSHEAD BREWPUB

114 J Street, Sacramento, 95814

TELEPHONE: (916) 443-BREW
DIRECTIONS: FROM I-5, TAKE THE J STREET EXIT AND FOLLOW THE SIGNS FOR OLD SACRAMENTO. THE BREWPUB IS LOCATED NEAR THE CORNER OF SECOND AND EYE, HALF A BLOCK FROM THE PONY EXPRESS STATUE.
HOURS: MON–THUR, SUN: 11:30A.M.–11P.M.; FRI–SAT: TILL 2A.M.
WHEELCHAIR ACCESS: YES
SMOKING: SMOKING AREA
ENTERTAINMENT: LIVE MUSIC THUR–SAT, JUKEBOX, TV, POOL, DARTS, CHESS
TOURS: ON DROP-IN BASIS, APPOINTMENTS ADVISABLE
PARKING: ON STREET (METERED), OFF-STREET (VALIDATED)
CREDIT CARDS: NONE

You've heard of the little piggie who went to market and the one who stayed home. Here is the little piggie who became famous. Hogshead Brewpub is well known for its unique theme which runs throughout the decor, the brews, and the food.

The entrance is misleading but makes for a fun discovery. The building boasts residence in Old Sacramento, the end of the line for the Pony Express. A few doors down from the monument to those dashing riders is an 1800s building with elegant wood-trim glass doors and fan-shaped windows above. But step inside and you greeted by the mural of a decidedly unelegent little piggie rolling kegs down a ramp—while another little piggie, probably the one who cried all the way home, flees ahead.

Down the stairway, with its old wooden railing, is the pub, whose floor, bar, tables, chairs, and booths all glow with the warm patina of hardwood. The walls are exposed brick. Hogshead displays several collections: a wide array of beer bottles, paper money from around the world, and a unique collection of taps with the handles carved in the shape of a hog's head or, appropriately, an apple. There are also video games, a big-screen TV, darts, and a pool table.

The menu boasts a lovely picture of, you guessed it, a hog's head with "In Hogs We Trust" emblazoned across the top. Inside you will find a fairly standard list of appetizers, snacks, soups, salads, and sandwiches. Of course, there is a sausage plate, veal, and kielbasa, served on a bed of spinach and topped with veal sauce, with German potato salad and sauerkraut. Salads and sandwiches are only served during lunch.

Then there is the Hogsheaven Pizza, which can be topped with a choice of ground sausage, pepperoni, ham, fresh mushrooms, olives, bell peppers, fresh tomatoes, onions, and three kinds of cheese. Rumor has it that the moniker is appropriate.

THE BREWS

Hogshead opened in the summer of 1986 by brewing pioneer Jim Schlueter, and it was the first brewpub to open in the Sacramento valley. Phil Salmon, with a background in the bar and restaurant business, bought it in 1988 and also became the brewmaster.

The system was built from scratch by Schlueter, with a five-gallon brewhouse and eight-barrel fermenters. Phil uses exclusively American malts, milled at the brewery and Cascade hop pellets. All of the beers are filtered. In 1994 he produced about five hundred barrels.

Three beers are always on tap, and they are available in twelve-ounce mugs ($2.00), sixteen-ounce pints ($2.50), liter mugs ($4.50), and pitchers ($7.00). Two-and-a-half-ounce samplers sell for 50¢. Party pigs are available for take out.

Hogshead Lager is light, refreshing, and slightly sour. Hogshead Pale Ale has a dry, fruity, malty character with sour notes. McSchlueter Dark Ale has a medium-roasted malt palate with fruity and sour notes. The bar also offers an array of bottled imports and craft beers.

RIVER CITY BREWING CO.

545 Downtown Plaza #1115, Sacramento, 95814

TELEPHONE: (916) 447-BREW;
FAX, 448-7153
DIRECTIONS: FROM I-5, TAKE THE J STREET EXIT, TURN LEFT AT THE SECOND LIGHT, AND RIGHT INTO THE DOWNTOWN PLAZA PARKING LOT.
HOURS: BAKERY & COFFEESHOP: DAILY, 7:30A.M.–CLOSING; BREWERY: SUN–WED: 11:30A.M.–11P.M.; THUR: TILL MIDNIGHT; FRIDAY–SAT: TILL 1:30A.M. (RESERVATIONS RECOMMENDED FOR PARTIES OF SIX OR MORE)
WHEELCHAIR ACCESS: YES
SMOKING: NO SMOKING INDOORS
ENTERTAINMENT: LIVE MUSIC ON OCCASION, TV
TOURS: ON A DROP-IN BASIS; APPOINTMENTS PREFERRED
PARKING: OFF-STREET, VALIDATED
CREDIT CARDS: AMEX, DINERS CLUB, MASTERCARD, VISA

In its first year in business, River City Brewing has garnered three coveted awards—"best beer selection" by *Sacramento Magazine*, "best new restaurant" by the California Restaurant Association and "best service" by the *Sacramento Bee*. So be prepared for some pleasant surprises.

River City Brewing is located in the remodeled Downtown Plaza on the ground level, affording a pleasant view of the open courtyard and access to patio dining. The surprise comes in the fact that it is not the typical brightly lit, noisy fast-food chain found in many malls. With over nine thousand square feet, it is modern, open, and inviting. The kitchen and oak-fired pizza oven entice the appetite, while glass windows wrap the interior in diffused sunlight and high ceilings offer a view of the dining balcony and the brewery. At the entrance is a display case filled with wonderfully decadent desserts fresh from the bakery. But then—just in time!—the elegant balcony railing with its barley motif catches your attention and draws you upward into a delightful dining experience.

The menu reads like a "Catalog of Everything Wonderful." Starters include Florida rock shrimp sundae, beer and onion soup with Muenster cheese, and Dungeness crab wild rice cakes. The dinner menu tempts the palate with pizzas such as the flatbread cheese pizza—turkey beer sausage, mushrooms, apples, onions, Gruyere, and honey mustard.

The entrees offer other delicacies. Cowboy Pasta with Roasted Chicken features a mushroom medley, red chard, Mascarpone cheese, and "Wild West" sauce. For the serious meat-eater, there is wood-grilled black Angus New York steak on smashed potatoes, with roast garlic sauce and crispy onions. If the entrees sound too filling, there are salads, sandwiches, and "menu additions" created especially for lunch. Whether the choice is a grilled burger, spicy eggplant with creamy polenta and garlic-cheese croutons, or a beer-battered catfish sandwich, served with chipotle aioli, a cup of corn hominy stew, and a green salad, no one walks away dissatisfied.

But wait. Before escape is possible, those aforementioned wonderfully decadent desserts must be confronted, such as chocolate mousse with cranberry sauce and white chocolate ganache. Or, just give in and visit the bakery for the complete tour! Finish your meal off with coffee—several varieties from espresso to Spanish mocha—or a nice after-dinner wine.

THE BREWS

Since it opened in November 1993, River City's wonderful cuisine has been complemented by beers of equal stature. This is due to the genius of brewmaster Luke DiMichele and brewer Roy Rudebusch. Luke is a graduate of the brewing school at the University of California at Davis and he came to River City from the Bricktown Brewery in Oklahoma City. Roy came up through the ranks of homebrewers. They are brewing with a fifteen-barrel system made by Century Manufacturing. Luke and Roy concentrate on traditional German lagers, using a decoction mash, bottom-fermenting yeasts, cold conditioning, and a mixture of American, Munich, and Vienna malts and American and German hops. For the ales, they use a portion of British malts and East Kent Golding hops. As a further example of their dedication to authentic, flavorful beers, the Pale Ale and many of the specialty beers are dry hopped and the darker beers are served unfiltered. Output in 1994 was fourteen hundred barrels, all sold on the premises.

Normally, five beers are on tap. Beers are available in .3-liter ($2.50) and half-liter ($3.50) servings. Samplers sets of four ounces of each go for $3.75. Take-out beer is available in gallon cubes.

The Pilsner (1.052) is a bright gold that sparkles with activity. It has a sweet, malty entry with a fresh, hoppy-tangy finish and lingering, dry hop bitterness. River City Lager (1.050), in the Munich helles style, is bright gold with a sweet malty palate balanced by tangy hops. The Vienna (1.056) is a dark amber with a tasty, roasted malt palate. The Pale Ale (1.054) is copper colored with an uncharacteristic sweet, malty palate. The cask-conditioned Oatmeal Stout (1.060) is black with a pleasant, roasted malt palate and notes of coffee and chocolate. They also have a Hefe Weizen (1.054), made with 60 percent wheat malt, and a Dopplebock (1.078).

Rubicon Brewing Co.

2004 Capitol Avenue, Sacramento, 95314

TELEPHONE: (916) 448-7032
DIRECTIONS: From I-80 (Business), take the Sixteenth Street exit; go north on Sixteenth and turn right on Capitol Avenue; it's on the corner of 20th and Capitol
HOURS: Mon–Thur: 11:30 a.m.–11:30 p.m.; Fri: till 12:30 a.m.; Sat: 9 a.m.–12:30 a.m.; Sun: 9 a.m.–10 p.m.
WHEELCHAIR ACCESS: Yes
SMOKING: None
ENTERTAINMENT: TV
PARKING: On street (pay)
CREDIT CARDS: Amex, MasterCard, Visa

How has the Rubicon Brewing Company managed to maintain such a loyal following in a city that offers so many choices to beer lovers? It's not in a touristy area, not in a popular mall, nor has it won any awards for design. What Rubicon offers is well-made beers in comfortable surroundings that regulars can call a home away from home—the best things in life are so simple!

Rubicon Brewing resides on a tree-lined street inhabited by offices, shops, cafes, and ethnic restaurants. With a white modern exterior, Rubicon is a truly "California" dining establishment whose interior features open ceilings, corrugated metal walls, and a curving, stainless-steel bar. Multipaned windows inside offer an excellent view of the brew tanks, or take a walk down the back hallway for a step-by-step look at the brewing process.

The locals seem to approve, since a true cross-section of folks regularly gathers for the good food and good times. Rubicon has dubbed the usually dead Monday night "Grateful Dead Night," inviting patrons to bring their tapes and turn the music up. On other nights, the music is rock, oldies, jazz, country—in fact, something for just about everyone.

The menu offers traditional pub fare at fair prices. There is a fine selection of sandwiches as well as chicken fajitas. If you like burgers, try the quarter-pound Bubba's Burger, or really test your capacity and go for the half-pound Ultimate Burger. There are also several salads and soups, including fresh soup of the day and an irresistible french onion soup.

The appetizers could be a meal by themselves. They even have two versions of wings: the Rubicon Wings are hot and spicy, served with carrot sticks and blue cheese dressing, and the Western Wings are deep-fried, tossed in beer-barbecue sauce and served with celery sticks and carrot sticks with blue cheese dressing. Whether it's for the music, the friendly staff, the food, the beer, or just to see who shows up on Monday nights, Rubicon Brewing Company is worth the drive, worth the stop, and absolutely worth the time.

THE BREWS

When Rubicon Brewing was under construction, Phil Moeller just showed up one day to help build the brewery. His background as an award-winning homebrewer combined with his hard work and eagerness to be part of the operation convinced owner Ed Brown to make Phil head brewer. When the brewery opened in 1987, Phil's Amber Ale took Sacramento by storm. Since then, Phil has received a master's degree in fermentation science from the University of California at Davis.

The beers are made in a ten-barrel system that has been expanded with extra fermenting and serving tanks. The beers are normally filtered, although they will occasionally do an unfiltered specialty beer. They use American two-row pale malt and a combination of domestic and British specialty malts, all milled at the brewery. Primarily American pellet hops are used, although an Irish hop is used for the Luck of the Irish, and East Kent Goldings are used in the stouts. The Luck of the Irish is dry hopped, as well as many of the specialty beers.

Beers are available in half pints ($1.50), pints ($2.25), and pitchers ($7.25). One-gallon beer boxes are available for take out. Usually six beers are on tap at a time.

I found Rubicon beers to be extremely clean, well made, and tasty. Rubicon Wheat (1.047) is bright gold and is light and refreshing. Rubicon Amber Ale (1.050) is a deep, reddish copper with a malty-fruity palate and a rich, hoppy-malty, tangy finish. Rubicon India Pale Ale (1.057) is bright amber with a fresh Cascade aroma and a long, hoppy finish—a terrific brew. Luck of the Irish (Irish red ale) is cloudy, amber to red, with a yeasty aroma and an absolutely delicious, fresh, fruity palate—sweet to start, stretching into a long, well-balanced dry malt and hop finish. Flanders Belgian Ale is a cloudy amber with a complex and tart palate of cloves, citrus, and apples. The Rubicon Stout (1.053) is dark brown to black with a dry, roast aroma and palate—the well-balanced finish is very rich with deeply roasted malt, hop bitterness, and notes of coffee. Winter Wheat Wine is a dark amber to light copper with an intense, sweet roasted malt palate and a full, almost syrupy body. It has a very bitter finish, an alcoholic warming, and tangy-fruity notes—a delightful barleywine.

The IPA took a gold medal at the 1989 and 1990 GABF. In addition, the Stout won a bronze at the 1990 festival, and their Raspberry Wheat (no longer made) won a bronze at the 1989 GABF.

Sutter Brewing Co.

6300 Folsom Boulevard, Sacramento, 95819

TELEPHONE: (916) 457-2337; (800) 273-9488; FAX, 457-8641
DIRECTIONS: From Hwy 50, take the 65th Street exit; the brewery is within a block of the exit
HOURS: Sun–Thur: 11a.m.–midnight; Fri–Sat: till 2a.m.
WHEELCHAIR ACCESS: Yes
SMOKING: No smoking inside
ENTERTAINMENT: Live music Mon–Wed (light jazz, blues, acoustic, conversational level), TV, electronic darts, board games
TOURS: On a drop-in basis
PARKING: Off street (free)
CREDIT CARDS: Amex, Diners Club, Discover, MasterCard, Visa

Sacramento has one of the highest concentrations of breweries in California. River City (now closed) came first, followed by Hogshead, then Rubicon, and the new River City after that. The newest entry in the Sacramento brewing scene is Sutter Brewing, which opened on Saint Patrick's Day 1995, in the east end of town.

The brewpub is very open and modern with a windowed facade looking onto bustling Folsom Boulevard. The long mahogany bar against the back of the room is one of the longest bars in Sacramento. Behind the bar, and taking up the entire back wall of the great room, the handsome stainless-steel and copper-clad brewery is exhibited behind glass. To the right is the dining area, and to the left is the lounge area and dart room. The walls are white and feature very large, colorful logos of the beers. Under the high ceilings hangs the exposed ductwork, painted bright red.

The menu offers a diverse variety of items; almost everything listed is priced under $6.00. Appetizers include Buffalo wings, fried calamari, and beer-battered mushrooms. Entrees include pizza, pasta, grilled sandwiches, burgers, chili, and salads. Vegetarian items are offered as well.

THE BREWS

The beers at Sutter's are made by brewmaster Jeff Blake with a fourteen-barrel, Pub Brewing system. Jeff got interested in good beer and brewing while studying geology at the University of Colorado at Boulder. After graduation, he went to the University of California at Davis, where he graduated from the master brewer's program. Before coming to Sutter, Jeff apprenticed at Rubicon Brewing for over a year.

The beers are made using all American, two-row pale and specialty malts and seasoned with domestic and imported leaf hops. Several of the beers are dry hopped. All of the beers are filtered.

Servings range from twelve-ounce glasses ($2.25) to pints ($2.75) and pitchers ($9.25). Sampler sets of four to six beers cost $2.75. There is beer to go in half-gallon jugs. The owners plan to distribute in the Sacramento area in kegs.

Jeff's four regular beers are Comstock Golden, American Red, Blueberry Wheat, and Irish Stout. Two specialties are also on tap, and Jeff plans to invite local homebrewers in as guest brewers. Sutter Brewing is so new that I have not had a chance to sample the beers, but I look forward to it with anticipation.

BREWERY AT LAKE TAHOE

3542 Lake Tahoe Boulevard, South Lake Tahoe, 96150

TELEPHONE: (916) 544-BREW; FAX: 544-7359
DIRECTIONS: AT U.S. HIGHWAY 50 & HAM LANE; BETWEEN SKI RUN BOULEVARD AND JOHNSON BOULEVARD
HOURS: DAILY: 11A.M.–CLOSING
WHEELCHAIR ACCESS: YES
SMOKING: NONE
ENTERTAINMENT: TV
TOURS: BY APPOINTMENT
PARKING: PARKING IS SCARCE
CREDIT CARDS: AMEX, DISCOVER, MASTERCARD, VISA

Your first glimpse of the Brewery at Lake Tahoe is of a typical ski-resort shop. Inside, the decor is California mission-style, with soaring ceilings, high rectangular windows, and exposed cross beams. There is a large expanse of white walls and ceilings with wood trim. Ceiling fans keep the air moving. The original building was tiny, with only the bar, a few tables and chairs, and a shelf attached to one wall. The expansion includes more of the same style decor with a granite fireplace. The bar in the original building is shaped like a question mark with the curve following the shape of one of the tanks. Some of the tap handles are ski tips, and the bar top is tooled copper reminiscent of early American pie safes. The view of the tanks is behind a half-brick, half-glass wall.

If you need more than a seat and conversation, the pub offers television, but the real entertainment in the area is snow-skiing and water sports. It is only ten minutes from Nevada's casinos and five minutes from the Heavenly Valley Ski Resort. The pub draws a pleasant mix of locals and tourists.

The menu is deli-style, with a full range of deli sandwiches and homemade chili. Their turkey burrito is worth mentioning, or you might want to try one of their hot dog creations. Other typical pub fare includes nacho platters, chicken wings ("very spicy hot"), and beer-steamed shrimp. They haven't forgotten their vegetarian friends, serving veggie versions of several items.

Whether you are on your way to the lake, skiing, or casinos, this is a great place to stop and smell the hops.

THE BREWS

Brewer Mike Doane was originally a bartender/manager when the brewpub opened in 1992 and took over the brewing operations when the original brewer left. He is brewing on a system put together with used, seven-barrel Grundy tanks. The beers are made from a base of malt extract, to which is added specialty grains that are steeped in hot water. American and Czech pellet hops are used. None of the beers are filtered.

Beers are available in half-pint servings ($1.95), pints ($3.25), two-pint mugs ($6.50), and pitchers ($9.95). The Bad Ass is priced slightly higher. Prices are lower during the daily happy hour (5:00–7:00 P.M.). Normally, six beers are available on tap at any given time. One-gallon beer boxes are available for take out.

Washer Wheat is a clear straw gold with a light malt palate with some tart/sour notes. Middle Peak Ale is bright gold with a sour palate. Alpine Amber is bright copper with a light, roasted malt palate. Paramount Porter is dark brown with plenty of deeply roasted malts. It is clean tasting with a rich, roasted malt finish. Bad Ass is hazy copper with a complex, slightly acidic, roasted malt and lightly hopped palate, followed by alcoholic warming. They have recently added an IPA.

BLUE WATER BREWING CO.

850 North Lake Boulevard, Tahoe City, 96145

TELEPHONE: (916) 581-2583; FAX, 581-1607

DIRECTIONS: AT THE NORTH END OF TOWN, ON HWY 28; IT'S IN THE LIGHTHOUSE SHOPPING CENTER, BEHIND SAFEWAY.

HOURS: DAILY: 11A.M.–1:30A.M.

WHEELCHAIR ACCESS: YES

SMOKING: NONE

ENTERTAINMENT: LIVE MUSIC (JAZZ, ROCK, R&B), POOL, DARTS

TOURS: ON A DROP-IN BASIS OR BY APPOINTMENT

PARKING: OFF-STREET (FREE)

CREDIT CARDS: MASTERCARD, VISA

Blue Water Brewing is located within eyesight of Lake Tahoe, which provided the inspiration for this brewpub's name. The incredible view of lake, mountain, and sky lifts the spirits. The exciting Western motif of the bar brings in this light and air with blond oak wainscoting, light pine furniture, bright green ductwork, and high ceilings. Indian rugs and a neon mural of Lake Tahoe and the mountains adorn the walls. There is an oval bar and a view of the brewing process through glass windows and doors. The furniture is all stool height set on deep blue carpeting.

They have recently added a stage with a dance floor and three new pool tables. There is a lot of glass and brass with track lighting and hanging lamps, providing an elegantly casual atmosphere. The room sports a display of local artwork, including steel and neon sculptures and photography. They have live entertainment on weekends featuring acoustic, rock, and R&B, and offer a special night: Tankard Tuesday with specials on pints and a "bring your own mug" discount, complete with live music. The owners and employees are friendly and eager to make your visit memorable.

Their appetizers are certainly memorable! Try the black bean potato skins, packed with drunken black beans and cheddar, or the chicken satay. Choosing is made even more difficult by cheese fries, calamari, and popcorn shrimp among other items. They offer a wide selection of salads. For a heavier meal, try a burger or the sausage sandwich—a flavorful sausage soaked in beer, grilled, and served on a sourdough roll with hot mustard.

Whatever you do, don't miss the beer chili, topped with cheddar cheese and cooled with sour cream; you choose whether you want it mild or atomic. They also offer fish & chips, veggie lasagna—a local favorite—and brewer's ribs. And finally, don't skip dessert: rum raisin bread pudding and "Mississippi mud" round out their excellent pub menu.

THE BREWS

Before becoming involved in craft brewing, brewmaster Phil Milbrand had a background in restaurant management, beer sales, and home-brewing. He worked at the Golden Pacific Brewery in Emeryville and was an assistant brewer at J & L Brewing in San Rafael just prior to coming to Blue Water.

Phil brews with a fifteen-barrel system manufactured by Pub Brewing. The water comes from Lake Tahoe, among the purest in the world. The malts are milled in house and include two-row domestic pale malt and English specialty malts. Nine different kinds of hop pellets from the Yakima Valley in Washington are used. The Arrowhead and the Sabertooth are dry hopped. All of the beers are filtered. Brewing began in March of 1994 and production reached a thousand barrels by the end of the year.

Five beers are on tap, including four regulars and one seasonal. They are available in eight-ounce servings ($1.75), pints ($3.00), yards ($8.00), and pitchers ($9.00). A set of samplers costs $4.50. Take out is available in half gallons, five-gallon kegs, and fifty-liter kegs.

The Palisades Pale (1.048) is bright gold with a fresh, dry malt aroma and a smooth, malty palate with notes of fresh hops in the finish. The Sabertooth India Pale Ale (1.066) is bright, deep gold with a clean, dry, and fresh hop palate. The Arrowhead Red (1.056) is bright copper with a perfumy aroma and a dry, roasted malt palate. Eagle Rock Raspberry, made with raspberry extract, is bright amber with a fresh raspberry aroma and palate. It has a good balance between the raspberry and the malt and has hoppy notes in the finish. Misty Mountain Oatmeal Stout (1.062) is black with a light brown, creamy head and a delicious mocha aroma. The palate is bitter, yet smooth, with good balance between the deeply roasted malts and hops and a creamy mouth feel. Other beers include an ESB, Scottish Ale, and The Kind (for Thanksgiving.)

TRUCKEE BREWING CO. & PIZZA JUNCTION
11401 Donner Pass Road, Truckee, 95734

TELEPHONE: BREWERY, (916) 587-5406; RESTAURANT, 587-7411
DIRECTIONS: DONNER PASS ROAD IS TRUCKEE'S MAIN STREET AND RUNS PARALLEL TO I-80. THE BREWPUB IS LOCATED ONE BLOCK WEST OF SAFEWAY. LOOK FOR THE TRAIN CARS IN THE PARKING LOT
HOURS: DAILY: 11A.M.–11P.M.
WHEELCHAIR ACCESS: YES
SMOKING: IN THE POOL ROOM
ENTERTAINMENT: TV, POOL, DARTS, VIDEO, HORSESHOES
TOURS: SAT: 1–4P.M. FROM MEMORIAL DAY TO LABOR DAY; ON A DROP-IN BASIS IF THE BREWER IS AVAILABLE
PARKING: OFF-STREET (FREE)
CREDIT CARDS: VISA

At an elevation of 5,897 feet, Truckee Brewing Company & Pizza Junction is the highest brewery in California. The beers are very clean tasting partially due to the fact that at such a high altitude and with such cold temperatures it's very difficult for wild yeast to grow.

The brewpub is easy to find—just look for the yellow caboose and the bright red boxcar that sit in the front parking lot. The caboose is brewer Jean Luc Gibassier's office and the boxcar serves as the lagering, bottling, and kegging room. Enter through the brick structure, which was once a school administration building.

The interior sports high ceilings, recessed lighting, and a wooden bar with marble trim. Behind four large windows is a view of the brewery. One wall is made of glass bricks, bringing in the California sun. The glassed-in sun porch with pot-belly stove provides warmth and welcome. There is a game room with video and pinball machines and a large pool room with five tables. There is a beer garden with a place to play horseshoes in the summer.

The regulars claim Truckee has the best pizza in town. Fresh dough is made daily, and only fresh vegetables and the best meats and cheeses are used. Start with homemade sauce and three cheeses, then add anything from chilies to Hawaiian pineapple to anchovies. Combination pizzas include vegetarian, the High Sierra (with ground beef, taco sauce, black olives, lettuce, tomato, and onions), and the Hot Lovers—spicy pepperoni pizza topped with hot or mild chili peppers.

They also offer charbroiled hamburgers and hot dogs, chicken sandwiches, and such pub fare as hot wings, fries, salad, onion rings, and soup. However, the special sauce in the spaghetti and lasagna make it difficult to try anything else, especially since they are served with delicious garlic bread. You can also get plenty of sauce in the meatball sandwich. For those who crave pasta without red sauce, they offer the John Scott special: spaghetti noodles smothered in mushrooms and garlic butter sauce and topped with parmesan cheese.

Whatever you choose, the food is all delicious, the atmosphere fun, and the trip up Donner Pass Road on the north shore of Lake Tahoe is worth the drive. Besides, where else could you tour a train car with a brewery inside?

THE BREWS

In 1985, Steve Downing added a small brewery to his restaurant, the Pizza Junction. Initially, he was making beer in five-gallon batches. In 1990 a new, seven-barrel system, designed by Steve and manufactured in Grass Valley, was added, and Jean Luc Gibassier from Strassbourg, France, became brewmaster. At the time, Jean Luc had no background in brewing, but he did plenty of reading and learned from Steve on the job.

The brewery makes lagers exclusively, using a five-step mashing cycle and aging for a minimum of three weeks. A combination of domestic two- and six-row pale malts and specialty malts are used. Leaf Chinook and Mount Hood hops are used. The beers are filtered. In 1994, eleven hundred barrels were produced, of which 20 percent was sold in the pub. Twenty-two-ounce bottles are distributed in the Reno, Carson City, and Lake Tahoe area.

Three beers are on tap at all times—Truckee Amber, Truckee Dark, and Boca Bock—and are dispensed from kegs. The beers are available in twelve-ounce ($1.50) and pint glasses ($2.50), and pitchers ($7.50). Being lagers, they are served very cold. Samplers are available for $3.00. Twenty-two-ounce bottles are available for take out.

Truckee Amber (1.050) is bright gold with a light hop aroma and a light fruity, musty-sour, hop palate. Truckee Dark (1.050) is brownish copper with a medium roasted malt palate. Boca Bock (1.068) is deep reddish-copper with a rich and complex malty palate. It is named after the first lager brewery in California, which opened in 1876 about five miles east of Truckee.

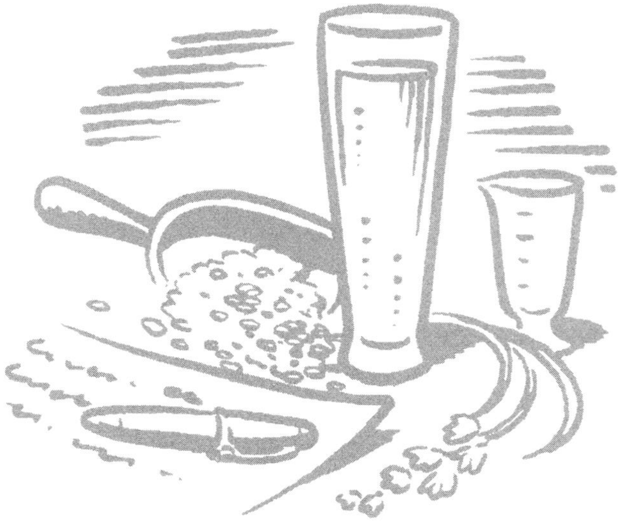

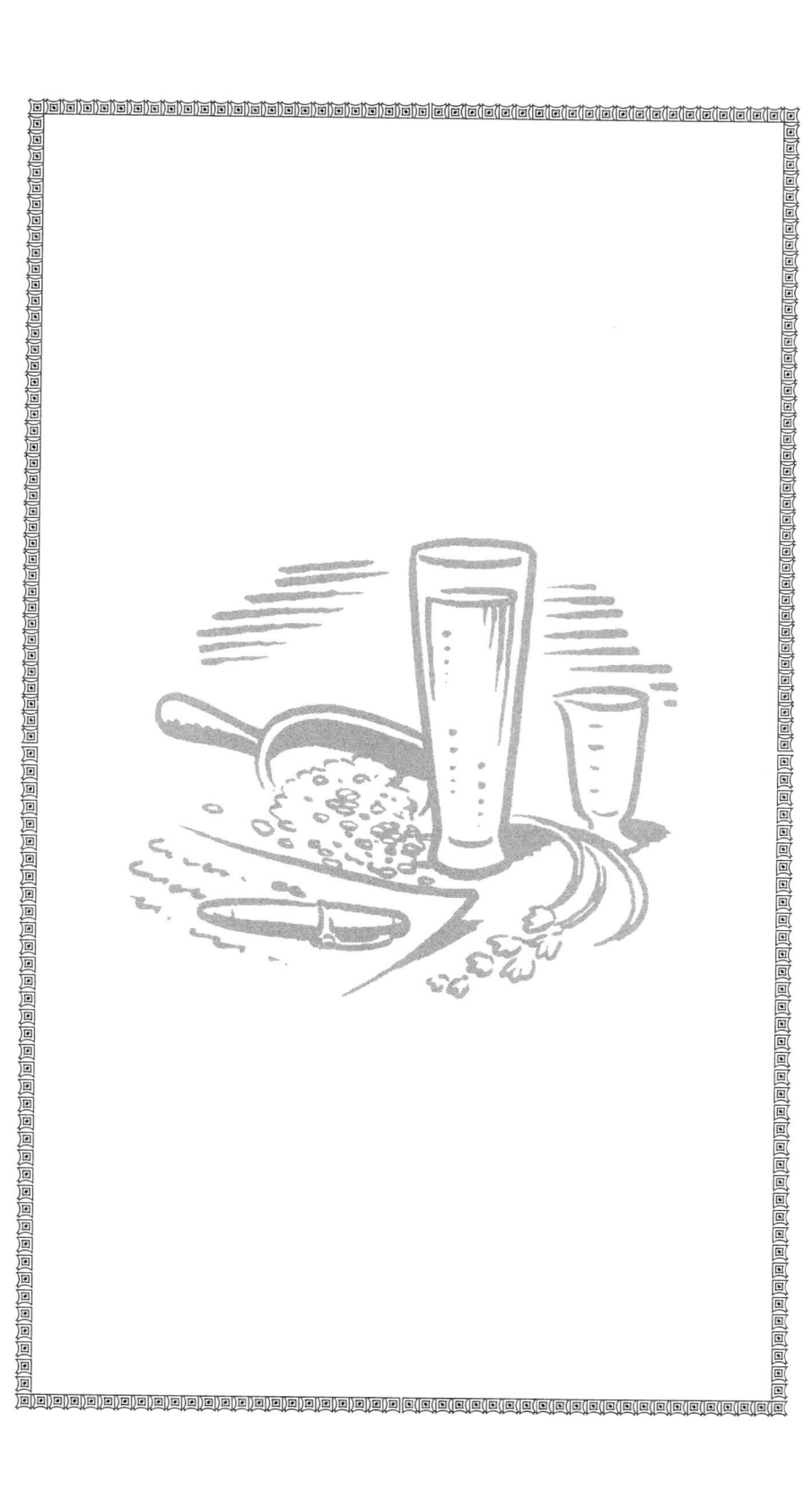

Beer Festivals

A good way to find out what's out there, without actually going to the brewery, is to attend a beer festival, where you can sample the beers, rub elbows with fellow beer lovers, and talk to someone from the brewery. Here is a listing of some festivals in northern California. For specific dates and other details, read the *Celebrator Beer News*.

One festival deserves special mention. The Great American Brew Festival (GABF) is hosted each fall in Denver by the Association of Brewers. All American breweries (craft breweries, brewpubs, and contract breweries) are invited to participate. With the price of admission, the public is allowed to try the more than 1,000 brands of beer offered in two-ounce samples. A panel of professional judges evaluates the beers according to beer style, awarding gold, silver, and bronze medals in each category.

APRIL	Microbrew & Apple Blossom Festival, Santa Rosa, Ives Park
MAY	Clovis Central California Brewfest, Clovis Annual Brew Ha Ha, Half Moon Bay Annual Beebop & Brew, Arcata
JUNE	Brewfest, San Rafael Haywood Brews & Brew, Haywood BeerFest at Saint Mary's College, Moraga
JULY	KQED International Beer & Food Festival, San Francisco, Concourse Exhibition Center California Small Brewers Festival, Tied House Brewing, Mountain View
AUGUST	Blues Brew Fest in the Park, Concord Tahoe Fat-Tire Micro Festival, Lake Tahoe
SEPTEMBER	Micro Brew & Blues Festival, Fairfield

Further Reading

The following brewery guidebooks are available to the beer lover. To locate copies, check your local bookstore. Four northern California brewpubs maintain excellent book collections in their gift shops: North Coast in Fort Bragg, Mendocino in Hopland, Anderson Valley in Boonville, and St. Stan's in Modesto.

America's Best Beers by Christopher Finch and W. Scott Griffiths (Little, Brown, Boston, 1994)

California Brewin' by Jack Erickson (RedBrick Press, Sonoma, CA, 1993)

The Guzzler's Guide to California Beer by Nancy Salcedo (Stinson Beach, CA, 1993)

On Tap: A Field Guide to North American Brewpubs and Craft Breweries by Steve Johnson (On Tap Publications, Clemson, SC, 1995)

Books are nice, but they cannot possibly keep up with the rapidly changing beer scene. A newsletter and a "brewspaper" are published to keep the consumer up to date.

The Celebrator Beer News, published bimonthly and available free from almost any California brewery, good beer bar, or good beer retail store.

What's On Tap, published nine times a year (send $25 to P.O. Box 7779, Berkeley, CA 94707).

Glossary

ADDITIVE—chemicals such as enzymes, preservatives, and antioxidants that are added to simplify the brewing process or prolong shelf life.

ADJUNCT—fermentable, unmalted grain, including wheat, corn, rice, or oats, used in addition to the malted barley. In the United States the larger breweries have used adjuncts extensively to lighten the flavor and body of their beers.

ALCOHOL—an intoxicant created through the fermentation process. Alcohol content is expressed as a percentage of the volume or weight of the beer.

ALL-GRAIN—an adjective describing the brewing process in which the brewer begins with grist, as opposed to using malt extract.

ALL-MALT—an adjective describing beer made with malted barley and without adjuncts.

BARLEY—a cereal grain used in making beer.

BARREL—a measure of beer; 31 gallons. When I say a "seven-barrel system," for example, I am not referring to the number of brewing vessels, but to the quantity of beer produced in each batch.

BEER—a fermented beverage made from malted cereal grain.

BOTTLE CONDITIONED—unpasteurized beer, naturally carbonated in the bottle.

BREWERIANA—beer-related memorabilia.

BREWHOUSE—the equipment used to make beer.

BREW KETTLE—the vessel in which wort from the mash is boiled with hops. Also called a copper.

BREWPUB—an establishment that brews beer and sells it for consumption on the premises.

BRIGHT BEER TANK—see under conditioning tank.

CARBON DIOXIDE—a gas created from the fermentation process. Carbon dioxide gives beer its effervescence.

CASK—a closed, barrel-shaped container for beer. They come in various sizes and are now usually made of metal. The bung in a cask must be made of wood, which allows the pressure to be released from the fermenting beer and for natural carbonation.

CASK CONDITIONED—unfiltered, unpasteurized beer that is served under natural CO_2 pressure and served either with a hand pump or directly from the tap in the keg.

CONDITIONING TANK—a vessel in which beer is placed after primary fermentation, where the beer matures, clarifies, and and may be naturally or artificially carbonated. Also called a bright beer tank or secondary.

CONTRACT BEER—beer made by one brewery and then marketed by a different company calling itself a brewery. The latter uses the brewing facilities of the former.

FINING—a gelatin used to clear away yeast.

GRAVITY—see under specific gravity.

GRIST—malt that has been ground prior to mashing.

HAND PUMP—a device for dispensing draft beer using a pump operated by hand. The use of a hand pump allows cask-conditioned beer to be served without the use of pressurized carbon dioxide to force it up.

HARD CIDER—a fermented beverage made from apples.

HIGH GRAVITY—refers to the original gravity. See under specific gravity.

HOPS—seed cones (or flowers) that grow on the hop vine (the Latin name is *humulus lupulus*). Only cones from the female vine are used in making beer.

KEG—a closed, metal, barrel-shaped container for beer. It is usually pressurized and has a capacity of 15.5 gallons (half a barrel). A half keg (7.75 gallons) is referred to as a "pony keg."

KRAEUSEN—to add very young beer to mature beer just prior to packaging in order to create a naturally carbonated beer.

LAUTER—to drain off the hot liquid (wort) from the grist after it has been mashed. This is normally done through the use of a false bottom, or screen, in the mash-lauter tun.

LAUTER TUN—a tank used to sparge and lauter the mash. Since mashing, sparging, and lautering normally take place in the same tank, it is frequently referred to as the mash-lauter tun.

LIQUOR TANK—a tank used to store water (sometimes referred to by brewers as "liquor") for the brewing process. They may store either hot or cold water.

LOW GRAVITY—refers to the original gravity. See under specific gravity.

MALT—barley that has been soaked in water, allowed to sprout, and then dried.

MALTOSE—a water-soluble, fermentable sugar contained in malt.

MASH—to soak grist in hot water in order to convert the starch to sugar and to extract other solubles from the grist.

MASH TUN—a tank where grist is soaked in hot water. The process is called "mashing." "Mashing in" is the expression used to describe the process in which the grist and hot water enter the mash tun in a slurry.

MEAD—a fermented beverage made from honey.

MICROBREWERY—a brewery producing small amounts of beer. The upper limit of annual production has been variously set at ten, fifteen, and twenty thousand barrels.

PASTEURIZE—the application of heat to bottled, canned, or kegged beer in order to arrest the activity of microorganisms, including yeast and bacteria. Pasteurization was first developed by the French scientist Louis Pasteur, who conducted several studies on the pasteurization of beer. Pasteurization may be either flash pasteurization (usually for kegs) where the beer is held at a high temperature for less than a minute and then rapidly cooled, or tunnel pasteurization (usually for bottles) where the bottles go through a tunnel of hot water for up to an hour.

PUB—an establishment serving beer and sometimes other alcoholic beverages for consumption on the premises. A pub usually serves food as well. The term originated in England and is short for "public house."

REINHEITSGEBOT—a 1516 German purity law that declared that only water, malted barley, and hops could be used to make beer. Yeast was not officially included, since it was taken for granted. The purity law was amended later to allow malted wheat. The purity law was struck down in 1987 by the European Court for being protectionist in nature.

ROOM TEMPERATURE—the temperature of the surrounding air where the beer is stored, typically around 55°F (13°C). "Room temperature" is actually a misnomer; it refers to "cellar" temperature. Beer served at actual pub room temperature would be unappetizing.

SEASONAL BEER—a beer brewed at a particular time of the year, such as bock or winter warmer.

SERVING TANK—a tank from which beer is dispensed.

SPARGE—to spray the mash with hot water in order to extract wort.

SPECIFIC GRAVITY (s.g.)—a measure of beer's density in relation to the density of water, which is given a value of 1 at 39.2°F (4°C). When fermentation begins, the wort's density is measured—this is called original gravity (o.g.). The o.g. is always higher than 1 because of the solubles, such as maltose, that are suspended in it. As the yeast converts the maltose into alcohol the gravity drops, alcohol being lighter than water. When brewers are ready to serve, bottle, or keg their beer, they take a final gravity reading, known as the finishing gravity (f.g.). "Low gravity" and "high gravity" both refer to the original gravity of a brew. A high gravity brew tends to be stronger (i.e., more alcoholic) than a low gravity brew, but the final alcoholic content depends on the relationship between the original and finishing gravities. The higher the original gravity and the lower the finishing gravity, the stronger the finished product.

WORT—the sweet liquid which is created from the mashing and boiling process. When the wort is cooled and fermented, it is called beer.

YEAST—a microorganism of the fungus family. During the fermentation of beer, the yeast consumes maltose and in the process creates alcohol and carbon dioxide.

ZYMURGY—the science or study of fermentation.

LIST OF BREWPUBS AND CRAFT BREWERIES

American River Brewing Co.	138
Anchor Brewing Co.	61
Anderson Valley Brewery & Buckhorn Saloon	111
Barley & Hops Brewery, Blues Club & Smokehouse	78
Bison Brewing Co.	38
Black Diamond Brewing Co.	85
Blue Water Brewing Co.	161
Boulder Creek Brewing Co. & Boulder Creek Grill & Cafe	90
Brewery at Lake Tahoe	159
Buckhorn Saloon	111
Buffalo Bill's Brewery	46
Burlingame Station Brewing	42
Cafe Pacifica and Sankt Gallen Brewery	64
Calistoga Inn & Napa Valley Brewing Co.	114
Carmel Brewing Co.	98
Coast Range Brewing Co.	92
Dempsey's Ale House & Sonoma Brewing Co.	128
Downtown Joe's Brewery & Restaurant	125
El Dorado Brewing, Mount Aukum	144
El Dorado Brewing Co., Stockton	103
El Toro Brewing Co.	97
Etna Brewery	116
Faultline Brewing	81
Fremont Brewing Co.	44
Golden Pacific Brewing Co.	43
Gordon Biersch Brewing Co., Palo Alto	59
Gordon Biersch Brewery Restaurant, San Francisco	66
Gordon Biersch Brewery Restaurant, San Jose	72
Hangtown Brewery	147
Hogshead Brewpub	152
Humboldt Brewery Co.	108
Humes Brewing Co.	122
J & L Brewing Co.	54
Lagunitas Brewing Co.	130
Lind Brewing Co.	76
Los Gatos Brewing Co.	51
Lost Coast Brewery & Cafe	117

Mad River Brewing Co.	109
Marin Brewing Co.	48
Mendocino Brewing Co. & Hopland Brewery, Brewpub & Beer Garden	123
Moonlight Brewing Co.	133
Moylan's Brewery & Restaurant	55
Murphys Creek Brewing Co.	145
Napa Valley Ale Works	127
Nevada City Brewing Co.	146
North Coast Brewing Co.	119
Pacific Coast Brewing Co.	57
Pacific Hop Exchange Brewing Co.	56
Pacific Tap & Grill	79
Red White & Brew	150
River City Brewing Co.	154
Rubicon Brewing Co.	156
St. Stan's Brewery & Restaurant	95
San Andreas Brewing Co.	93
San Francisco Brewing Co.	68
Santa Cruz Brewing Co. & Front Street Pub	99
Santa Rosa Brewing Co.	131
Seabright Brewery Pub & Restaurant	101
Sierra Nevada Brewing Taproom & Restaurant	139
Sonoma Brewing Co.	128
Stoddard's Brewhouse & Eatery & Benchmark Brewery	83
Sudwerk Privatbrauerei Hübsch	142
Sutter Brewing Co.	158
Tied House Cafe & Brewery, Mountain View	53
Tied House Cafe & Brewery, San Jose	74
Tied House Pub & Pool, Alameda	36
Triple Rock Brewery & Alehouse	40
Truckee Brewing Co. & Pizza Junction	163
Tuscan Brewing Co.	149
Twenty Tank Brewing Co.	70